JIM GEORGE

A YOUNG MAN'S GUIDE TO DISCOVERING HIS BIBLE

HARVEST HOUSE PUBLISHERS
EUGENE, OREGON

Cover by Dugan Design Group, Bloomington, Minnesota

Cover photo © EDHAR / Shutterstock

A YOUNG MAN'S GUIDE TO DISCOVERING HIS BIBLE
Copyright © 2014 Jim George
Published by Harvest House Publishers
Eugene, Oregon 97402
www.harvesthousepublishers.com

Library of Congress Cataloging-in-Publication Data
    George, Jim
    A young man's guide to discovering his Bible / Jim George.
        pages cm
    Includes bibliographical references.
    ISBN 978-0-7369-6015-1 (pbk.)
    ISBN 978-0-7369-6016-8 (eBook)
    1. Bible—Textbooks. 2. Teenage boys—Religious life. 3. Christian teenagers—
Religious life. I. Title.
    BS605.3.G46 2014
    220.071'2—dc23

                                                                    2014007993

Printed in the United States of America

18 19 20 21 22 / VP-CD / 10 9 8 7 6 5 4 3 2

To the special young men in my family,

Jacob Seitz
Matthew Zaengle
Isaac Seitz
Ryan Zaengle

and all young men who want to know more about God.

Contents

1

Unlocking the Secrets of the Universe

*In the beginning God created
the heavens and the earth.*

Genesis 1:1

Zack is your average 15-year-old guy. He loves sports, playing video games, and isn't all that fond of school. Oh, he makes just enough effort to get by. His teachers are satisfied with his mediocre efforts—after all, he doesn't cause any problems for them. But that was about to change. Zack would soon be given a challenge that would rock his world forever.

Justin, the youth pastor at Zack's church, had asked Zack to drop by his office for a chat. Zack had no idea what Justin wanted to talk about. He couldn't think of anything he had done wrong. He pretty much approached the youth group the same way as he approached school: Don't make waves. Don't look or act too smart. Just blend in.

"Zack, I've had my eye on you ever since I took this position as youth leader," Justin began as soon as Zack entered the office. Zack's heart sank. On no—busted! His cover as an average, non-interested teen had just been blown.

"Zack," Justin continued, "I'd like to take you on a journey to unlock the secrets of the universe. Are you interested?"

Zack had spent his teen years trying not to care about anything. Well, except himself and his special interests and hobbies. But the challenge was tempting. He had always liked reading action and adventure books about quests and the search for mysterious artifacts and secret codes. So, without much thought, Zack blurted out, "Sure—what do I have to do?"

Ultimately, what Justin was really asking Zack was, "Would you like to discover the answers to the secrets of the universe? That is, would you like to understand your Bible?"

The Challenge

Suppose a friend or even a stranger came up to you and handed you a note that read, "The extent of something is in direct proportion to the sum of nothing divided by its separate parts." If you're like me, you would give the note a blank stare because, if there was a message packed within those words, the meaning of it wouldn't be very obvious.

Or how about receiving a note that read, "Alabby labbakayon Justinabokin"? Again, those are just random letters on a piece of paper with no understandable message.

Unfortunately, many teens regard the Bible as you would regard these two notes. The popular thinking is this: "The Bible is supposedly a message from God written with words you recognize, but whose meaning is mostly unclear and way beyond your understanding."

So you, like most boys your age, might believe you need an expert to explain God's message to you. Someone like a youth pastor or perhaps a Bible scholar. Or maybe you think you need to go to a Bible school for a couple years before you can really understand your Bible.

If you view the Bible as mostly unknowable, you might not have a very strong desire to read it. After all, it seems like a hard-to-understand collection of stories and mysterious sayings.

But is that really the case? Why would God give you a book about Himself that you and others cannot understand? The answer is that He didn't. God meant for men and women of all ages, including a teen like you, to be able to understand the Bible. It is necessary—no, make that essential—that you not wait until you are an adult to gain some understanding of the Bible. Nor is it necessary to wait for an expert to explain the Bible to you.

God wants you to know His Word...now. He wants you to understand what He is saying to you right now, so you can make the best kinds of choices right now! The sooner, the better. So the issue is not *can* you understand the Bible. The issue is do you *want* to understand the Bible?

It's totally up to you. If you are up for it—along with Zack— you can join him as he takes on Justin's challenge to go on a journey to unlock the secrets of the universe.

Your mission, my friend, is to understand your Bible.

"And why would I want to do that?" you might be asking. "What's so special about the Bible?"

Why Is the Bible So Special?

The Bible is the most priceless possession of the human race. Because the goal of this book is to help you discover and understand God's Word, go get your Bible now and write out the verses listed below as you answer the question, Why is the Bible so special?

1. The Bible is the most complete revelation of God to man—Ephesians 1:17.

_____

_____

_____

_____

Bonus: Write out the definition of the word *revelation* from a dictionary.

_____

_____

_____

2. The Bible is trustworthy—Psalm 119:138.

_____

_____

_____

3. The Bible is true—John 17:17.

_____

_____

_____

4. The Bible is eternal and therefore indestructible— Psalm 119:89.

_____

_____

_____

5. The Bible's message brings salvation—2 Timothy 3:15.

_____

_____

_____

6. The Bible's message brings spiritual maturity—Acts 20:32.

_____

_____

_____

7. The Bible's message is alive—Hebrews 4:12.

_____

_____

_____

8. The Bible's message applies to people of every race and of every age, male or female—Isaiah 51:8.

_____

_____

_____

9. The Bible's message has one great theme, Christ— Hebrews 13:8.

_____

_____

_____

How to Approach the Bible

Are you convinced yet that the Bible is important? Hopefully you are at least leaning toward seeing the Bible as something unique and special. At first glance, the Bible might look and feel like any other book. It has black words on white paper, just like other books. However, the Bible claims that God Himself inspired it. God spoke His message through more than 40 different authors over the course of hundreds of years to produce a specific message for all of mankind.

And even though it was written 2000 years ago and countless attempts have been made to destroy it, the Bible has survived and is the most popular book that has ever been printed. Men and women all over the world have given their lives and fortunes in order to possess even a small portion of the Bible.

These facts should make you stop and think. After all, if the Bible really is a message from God, wouldn't it be well worth your time to discover what it says? You will never know how significant the Bible is until you open it and begin to read it for yourself.

Take up the challenge along with Zack. If the Bible could possibly hold the answers to questions about the universe— including questions about the past, present, and future—why not start reading through as much of it as you can? Then if you think it still holds possibilities, you might want to add to your understanding by spending some time studying the Bible as you read. These two exercises, reading and studying, will be the most profitable efforts you can make each day for the rest of your life—starting with today and this week!

Here are some suggestions on how you can get to know your Bible better and use it. Once again, write out what the Bible says about itself.

1. Recognize the supernatural nature of the Bible— 2 Timothy 3:16.

_____

_____

_____

2. Realize the Bible's usefulness—2 Peter 1:3.

_____

_____

_____

3. Approach the Bible with a mind that is open to the truth—2 Timothy 2:15.

_____

_____

_____

4. Respond to the Bible's message—John 3:16.

_____

_____

_____

5. Resolve to live out the truths of the Bible—1 Samuel 12:24.

_____

_____

_____

6. Count on experiencing the blessings of knowing and obeying God's Word—Psalm 1:1-3.

_____

_____

_____

Getting Past Your English Class

If you asked most teen guys what two classes they detested the most in school, a good number of them would probably say, "English grammar and English literature!" Maybe that's why many people can't or won't read the Bible—because the Bible is grammatically constructed and it is literature. In fact, the Bible is made up of several different types of literature. It contains poetry, prophecy, teaching, allegories, and narrative (or, as your English teacher would call it, prose).

Much of the Old Testament, the Gospels (the books that tell the story of Jesus), and Acts is narrative. Narratives are stories, in this case God's story—a story that is utterly true and crucially important. Bible narratives tell you about things that happened—but not just ordinary things. Their purpose is to show God at work in His creation and among His people. The narrative honors God and helps you to understand and appreciate Him. Narratives give you a picture of God's care and protection along with providing illustrations of many other lessons important to your life.

Genesis, the very first book in the Bible, is a narrative, a story. Read the text of Genesis 1:1-5 below, then answer the questions that follow.

1 In the beginning God created the heavens and the earth.

2 Now the earth was formless and empty, darkness was over the surface of the deep, and the Spirit of God was hovering over the waters.

3 And God said, "Let there be light," and there was light.

4 God saw that the light was good, and he separated the light from the darkness.

5 God called the light "day," and the darkness he

called "night." And there was evening, and there was morning—the first day.

What is this story about?

_____

_____

_____

What does this story tell you about God?

_____

_____

_____

What answers do these verses give about the origin of the universe—about the creation of the world and all things?

_____

_____

_____

All narratives have a story line or plot and characters, whether divine, human, animal, vegetable, or whatever. However, the Old Testament narratives have plots that are all part of a bigger, special plan. They also have a special cast of characters, the most special of whom is God Himself. Let's follow up on what we just read in Genesis 1:1-5 and read Genesis 3:1-7 as an example.

¹ Now the serpent was more crafty than any of the wild animals the Lord God had made. He

said to the woman, "Did God really say, 'You must not eat from any tree in the garden'?"

2 The woman said to the serpent, "We may eat fruit from the trees in the garden,

3 but God did say, 'You must not eat fruit from the tree that is in the middle of the garden, and you must not touch it, or you will die.'"

4 "You will not certainly die," the serpent said to the woman.

5 "For God knows that when you eat from it your eyes will be opened, and you will be like God, knowing good and evil."

6 When the woman saw that the fruit of the tree was good for food and pleasing to the eye, and also desirable for gaining wisdom, she took some and ate it. She also gave some to her husband, who was with her, and he ate it.

7 Then the eyes of both of them were opened, and they realized they were naked; so they sewed fig leaves together and made coverings for themselves.

Who are the characters in this story?

_____

_____

_____

What was the story line, or the plot?

_____

_____

_____

What was the result of the man and woman's actions?

_____

_____

_____

Based on these verses, how would you answer if
someone asked you, "Where did sin come from?"

_____

_____

_____

Your Goal

Your goal in reading and studying the Bible is to first find
out what the Bible meant to the people who read it when it was
written.

Then ask yourself: Would God have two different messages—
one for the original readers, and another for today? The answer
is no, and that's one of the key reasons for Bible study: finding
out what the Bible's message was to the original readers, and
then taking that same message and applying it to your life today.

TAKING IT ALL IN

No one lives in a vacuum. You are and will always be influenced and impacted by people and your surroundings. Obviously, your parents have and will continue to provide the greatest contribution to your development. And as the years go by, there will be others. Maybe a coach, a pastor, a Sunday school teacher, a best friend, even a big brother.

And there will be some people who will provide a not-so-good influence. If you're not careful and wise, they can drag you down. How will you know if what you are experiencing from others or your surroundings is good for you?

God has provided for you in advance. He has already given you a way to evaluate your life experiences before they occur, before you are tempted. He has supplied you with a guidebook, the Bible. Yes, the Bible unlocks the secrets of the universe, but it is also meant to be the greatest and the most lasting influence in your everyday life. First you need to discover God's guidelines in the Bible—His wisdom and His do's and don'ts. God's Word can make you wise unto salvation, and it can serve as a light that will guide your steps along the road of life.

So what do you think? Are you ready to take the challenge along with Zack and start the quest to unlock the secrets of the universe? Then head to the next chapter, and see where it leads.

What Others Have Said About the Bible

I believe the Bible is the best gift God has ever given to man.
All the good from the Savior of the world
is communicated to us through this book.[1]

ABRAHAM LINCOLN
16th President of the United States

2

Do You Have the Code?

*The person without the Spirit does not accept
the things that come from the Spirit of God
but considers them foolishness,
and cannot understand them because
they are discerned only through the Spirit.*

1 CORINTHIANS 2:14

Zack left Pastor Justin's office not knowing what to think. Zack had spent most of his teen years trying to avoid being noticed. Yet to his surprise, the new youth pastor had not only noticed him but had given him a challenge—a challenge that intrigued Zack but also scared him. Pastor Justin wanted Zack to learn how to study the Bible!

In his heart, Zack wasn't sure he wanted to know what the Bible had to say. He knew there was something missing in his life, but didn't know for sure what it was. He also knew from Justin's Bible lessons at youth group that God was concerned about a person's conduct. Zack wasn't a bad person, but neither was he a perfect angel—just ask his parents! They would have easily been able to remember some of the things he had done wrong in the past.

So Zack was caught in a dilemma. He wanted to spend time with Justin because he was a really neat guy and fun to be around. But at the same time, Zack wasn't so sure he wanted to find out what the Bible might have to say about him and his actions.

But every time Zack read his Bible or heard someone teach from the Bible, he was mystified. He was pretty sure he wasn't dumb. Why, if he really wanted to, he could make straight *A*s in school—no problem! But when it came to figuring out the Bible and spiritual things, it was like he needed a code of some kind to help him understand what was being said.

Every day that week until his next meeting with Justin, Zack wrestled with these questions over and over.

The Natural Man

As it turns out, Zack's concern was well-founded. During his next meeting with Justin, the youth pastor began by talking about the spiritual nature of the Bible. Justin went on to explain the reason many people can't understand the Bible is because they are not Christians. Zack immediately told Justin that he was a Christian—he had raised his hand at a Christian youth camp after a message, and was told he was now a Christian. "Yes," he weakly reassured Justin, "I am a Christian." But he said this without much conviction.

Justin didn't seem to be totally convinced either, so he had Zack open up his Bible and read 1 Corinthians 2:14-16:

> 14 The person without the Spirit does not accept the things that come from the Spirit of God but considers them foolishness, and cannot understand them because they are discerned only through the Spirit.

> 15 The person with the Spirit makes judgments about all things, but such a person is not subject to merely human judgments,

16 for, "Who has known the mind of the Lord so
as to instruct him?" But we have the mind of Christ.

Of course Zack didn't understand what he had just read.
So Justin explained: "God teaches His people from the Bible
through the ministry of the Holy Spirit."

Justin went on: "The passage you just read talks about a 'person without the Spirit,' or 'the natural man.'[1] This person," Justin continued, "lacks the supernatural life and wisdom necessary to understand a spiritual book like the Bible.

"So, Zack, just to make sure you know what it means to be a Christian, I'm giving you some homework. Your mission is to understand something called the Romans Road because all the verses are from the book of Romans."

Zack winced at the mention of homework. But still he was curious about the Romans Road.

The Romans Road

Use the spaces below to copy the following verses from your Bible. Travel along with Zack as the author of these verses, the apostle Paul, leads you toward an understanding of what it means to have a relationship with God through His Son, Jesus Christ.

The Fact of Sin

Romans 3:23— _____

_____

_____

_____

What does Romans 3:23 say? We all were born with sin. You might not want to admit it, but you do have sin in your heart. If you have not received Christ as your Savior, you are under sin's influence and control. Oh, maybe you do a few good deeds once in a while, but unless you are perfect, you are still a sinner. A sinner is anyone who has broken any of God's commandments. Have you ever told even a little white lie? Everyone has—and that classifies you as a sinner.

Your response: Admit that you are a sinner.

The Penalty for Sin

Romans 6:23a—_____

_____

_____

_____

What does that passage mean? Sin is a dead-end street, and the penalty for sin is death. We all face physical death, but even worse is spiritual death—a death that separates you from God and lasts for all eternity.

Your response: Understand that you deserve death for your sin.

The Love of God

Romans 5:8—_____

_____

_____

_____

What does Romans 5:8 say? When Jesus, who was God in human flesh, died on the cross, He paid the penalty for our sins. He took all the sins of the world upon Himself on the cross, making it possible for Him to free you out of slavery to sin and death. The only requirement for this freedom—and forgiveness—is that you believe in Jesus and what He has done for you.

Your response: Give your life to God. He poured out His love for you through Jesus on the cross. Jesus is your only hope for forgiveness and change. His love made a way for you to no longer be a slave to sin. His love is what saves you—not religion or church membership or good deeds. God loves you!

The Free Gift of God

Romans 6:23b—_____

_____

_____

_____

What does that passage say? The love of God provides salvation as a free gift to you. You cannot earn this gift. You must desire it, reach out to God for it, and He will give it to you.

Your response: Ask God to forgive you and save you.

The Results of Salvation

Romans 10:9-10—_____

_____

_____

_____

What does Romans 10:9-10 say? Your salvation will produce two results: (1) Your belief in your heart that Jesus Christ is your Lord, (2) which will be expressed to others by your mouth, confirming your faith in Christ.

Your response: Tell others about Jesus.

Have you received Jesus into your heart? Have you put your trust in Him as your Savior? If not, or if you aren't sure, a prayer like this can help you take this most important step you will ever take in your life. When you take this step, you receive salvation, the forgiveness of sin, eternal life, and the ability to understand the Bible.

> Jesus, I know I am a sinner, and I want to turn away from my sins and follow You. I believe that You died on the cross for my sins and rose again, that You conquered the power of sin and death. I want to accept You as my personal Savior. Come into my life, Lord Jesus, and help me understand Your Word, the Bible, so I can follow You. Amen.

Saying these words won't make you a Christian. But believing these words with all your heart will. So if you truly believe what you are reading above and you have prayed it sincerely, you are no longer a "natural man." You are now a Christian, a person who is capable of seeing and understanding spiritual truths.

And here's some really great news: Jesus has given you all the spiritual resources you need to understand the Bible because you now possess "the mind of Christ" (1 Corinthians 2:16).

A Desire to Grow

Have you ever thought about what life would be like if you failed to grow physically? Maybe you've already had a few major growth spurts, and you're nearly six feet tall. That wouldn't be such a terrible thing. But what if you never had any growth spurts? What if you ended up staying short like a little child? You wouldn't want that, would you? That would be devastating.

What is equally tragic is a young man who is a Christian who is not growing spiritually or whose spiritual growth has been stunted. If you are a child of God, the Lord expects you to grow spiritually as well as physically. In the Bible, growth is seen as a naturally occurring by-product of your life in Christ. Write out what God wants for you, His young Christian soldier:

2 Peter 3:18— _____

_____

_____

_____

The writer of the book of Hebrews also assumed that, with the passing of time, his readers would grow to the point where they could be teaching others the basics of God's Word. Take a look at this verse in your Bible and write out God's rebuke to His readers because they failed to grow.

Hebrews 5:12— _____

_____

_____

_____

Spiritual Junk Food

You know what sin is, right? It's anything that displeases a holy God. Read the following verse, then circle the kinds of actions that God wouldn't want you to do:

> Rid yourselves of all malice and all deceit, hypocrisy, envy, and slander of every kind (1 Peter 2:1).

What action does God want you to take?

_____

_____

_____

Here are quick definitions for each of these sinful actions:

Malice means desiring to inflict harm or suffering on
   another person.
Deceit means concealing or altering the truth.
Envy means wanting what someone else has.
Slander means making false or evil statements about
   another person.

That is a nasty list, isn't it? I think we can compare these activities to eating junk food and its effect on your appetite. As a physically growing teen, what are you constantly looking for in the refrigerator? Pretty obvious, isn't it? You're always hungry for food. Real food—the kind that will fuel your growth.

But what happens when you eat junk food right before lunch or dinner? You're no longer hungry for the real food, the good stuff.

The same is true in your spiritual life. Participating in sins like those listed in 1 Peter 2:1—the junk food—dulls your desire for what's spiritually healthy, what the Bible and God prescribe for you. But if you do what God asks and rid yourself of these sins, what will happen according to 1 Peter 2:2?

Like newborn babies, crave pure spiritual milk, so that
by it you may grow up in your salvation.

_____

_____

_____

Look again at 1 Peter 2:1. If you want to crave and benefit from "spiritual milk" or food, what must you do first?

_____

God Is Looking for a Few Good Men

The Marine Corps is made up of an elite band of men who have volunteered their services for many tough responsibilities. The desire to be a Marine prompts many young men, not much older than you, to become part of this select group. They are special and have been called upon many times to do missions that are beyond the capabilities of other military units.

God too is looking for young men who want to be special. He's on the lookout for those who desire to be part of His elite team and are willing to do what is necessary to qualify. I'm thinking you too want to be this kind of guy—the guy God wants you to be. I believe you want to be one of God's "few good men." How can you be this kind of man? By making sure you are growing spiritually strong. Want it, desire it, and do it. This means you need to make a few decisions.

1. *You must choose to read your Bible.* Why? Because this is where you meet with God. He speaks to you through His Word. Now, God isn't going to force you to spend time with Him. No, this is your decision. So you've got a serious choice to make.

You're probably thinking, *How can I spend time with God? I'm a busy guy!* Well, think about this: How much time do you spend playing video games, watching TV, or getting together with your buddies? Why not take some of this time and choose to spend it with God?

2. *You must choose to talk to God.* Any meaningful relationship requires that both parties communicate with each other. God speaks to you through His Word, the Bible, and you speak to Him through your prayers. Prayer isn't as hard as some people

think it is. It is nothing more than simply talking to God. You talk to your friends, don't you? Well, God wants to be your friend too. And He wants to help you make the right kinds of choices in life. So why not start talking to Him? Why not start asking Him for His advice and help? Hold on to this thought because we will be learning more about prayer in the next chapter.

3. *You must choose to confess your sin.* Jesus died to take away the penalty of sin. But your daily sins hinder your relationship with a holy God. Think of yourself as a pipe that the Holy Spirit flows through. But your sins clog that pipeline and the Holy Spirit cannot flow through you and empower you and help you.

Confession of sin is admitting you did something wrong. Your confession then restores your relationship with God, and the Holy Spirit once again flows freely through you to help you live for Jesus. Write out 1 John 1:9 and notice the results of confession:

_____

_____

_____

4. *You must choose to make some sacrifices.* Any truly great endeavor demands sacrifice. Nothing of substance happens without effort. The Christian life is one of willing sacrifice and commitment. It's no different than joining the Marines. When you join you are expected to make some serious sacrifices—a lot of them. God is asking for the same kind of commitment!

So what activities would you be willing to scale back or give up in order to gain something greater, to grow in your spiritual life? Would you be willing to...

...say no to some time watching TV,
...say no to playing some video games,
...say no to some time with friends,
...say no to some time playing sports?

Jesus said, "Whoever wants to be my disciple must deny themselves and take up their cross and follow me" (Matthew 16:24). Are you up for a greater level of commitment? For making some sacrifices so you can follow Jesus? If you are, then you are just the kind of guy God is looking for!

TAKING IT ALL IN

How was your journey down the Romans Road? If you are already a Christian, I hope it was a good review.

But if the Romans Road journey was a new revelation for you and you realized you weren't a Christian, I hope you accepted God's offer of eternal life through Jesus Christ. If you made this decision, tell someone what you did—maybe a parent or your church youth leader, or the person who gave you this book.

For Zack, the truths in the Romans Road were a wake-up call, and he prayed to receive salvation through Jesus Christ. Then he immediately called Justin, his youth pastor, and told him the good news.

Zack was so excited to finally figure out what had been missing in his life—a relationship with Jesus. He was looking forward to understanding God's Word through his new eyes— "spiritual eyes." He now possessed the "code" to understanding the Bible and the secrets of the universe!

What Others Have Said About the Bible

In all my perplexities and distresses,
the Bible has never failed
to give me light and strength.

ROBERT E. LEE
Commanding General of the South in the US Civil War

3

Using Your Secret Weapon

In every situation,
by prayer and petition, with thanksgiving,
present your requests to God.

PHILIPPIANS 4:6

Zack's call made Pastor Justin's day. He was ecstatic when Zack shared the news that he had become a Christian, a believer in Jesus Christ. Justin prayed for Zack over the phone and asked God to continue to confirm His presence in Zack's life. They both hung up from the call looking forward to their next meeting.

The Christian life is an exciting but challenging journey, and it's not often that someone can help a new Christian get started on it. But that's exactly where Justin found himself. Zack was standing at the starting line of his new life in Jesus. As Zack was poised and ready to spring forward into a race that would last a lifetime, Justin was ready to help him get started on the right foot.

"Well," Justin noted as Zack entered his office, "I can see you're ready to continue on your quest. Are you ready to learn about a secret weapon you'll need along the way?"

Yes, Zack was ready and raring to go. It was like a fog had been lifted from his mind and he was starting to see and understand the Bible more clearly. Even the things their pastor preached on Sunday mornings now made sense, which took Zack by surprise. With eager anticipation, Zack settled down in the chair next to Justin's desk with an expectant look, feeling like a baby bird waiting to be fed.

Running the Race

Justin then had Zack open his Bible. He took Zack to one of his favorite passages—1 Corinthians 9:24-27. Justin began to read it out loud:

> 24 Do you not know that in a race all the runners run, but only one gets the prize? Run in such a way as to get the prize.
>
> 25 Everyone who competes in the games goes into strict training. They do it to get a crown that will not last, but we do it to get a crown that will last forever.
>
> 26 Therefore I do not run like someone running aimlessly; I do not fight like a boxer beating the air.
>
> 27 No, I strike a blow to my body and make it my slave so that after I have preached to others, I myself will not be disqualified for the prize.

After Justin finished reading the passage, he paused for a moment, then began to explain its historical background. "In the days of the apostle Paul, the writer of the book of 1 Corinthians, the ancient Greeks observed two great athletic events—the Olympic Games and the Isthmian games. Paul saw the idea of running a race as a good analogy for describing a believer's usefulness to God. In the same way that the very best athletes were committed to giving their best, we as Christians need the same kind of commitment so we can run the Christian race well."

Justin then shared with Zack about what he needed as he ran this race. A Christian must have self-control. As Paul said in verse 25, "everyone who competes in the games goes into strict training." That's the key to success. The phrase "strict training" refers to self-control, or the idea of strength under control.

You know from personal experience that a young man needs to have self-control. There are many areas in life in which a guy's life can spin out of control.

Physical areas—Your body is the temple of the Holy Spirit (1 Corinthians 6:19) and must be treated with care and respect. It's not your body—it's God's. Therefore, you are not to abuse it through overeating, using drugs, smoking cigarettes, or drinking alcohol. Use the following statement as your guide in the physical area: Whatever cannot be managed with self-control is an addiction. The best thing you can do is determine to never start abusing your body.

Emotional areas—A guy needs to show the right kind of emotions, like love and caring. Indifference is not an option for a Christian. Jesus cared about the people around Him, and so should you, especially when it comes to your family—even your little brother or sister. Outbursts of the wrong kinds of emotions, and yelling and displaying a temper, must be checked and discarded. God doesn't want us to be like a smoldering volcano in our heart and to be ready to erupt at the slightest provocation.

Sexual areas—The world offers many choices that make it easy for a young man to be out of control with pornography and lustful thoughts and temptations. A lack of sexual control now can destroy a young man's future relationships and other things.

Running the Race with Focus

As Paul wrote in 1 Corinthians 9:25-26, a Christian must have focus. A bit earlier in verses 19 and 22, we see that Paul's focus was the salvation of the lost. That was his goal in life. He ran his race "not...like someone running aimlessly." A young man like you must also have this same intense focus—not only for the lost people around you, but on your own spiritual and mental growth.

You are not too young to be thinking about your future. You need to be asking questions like, "What are God's plans for my life? How can I prepare and educate myself?"

Here's another question to get you thinking along these lines: What do you want to achieve by the time you finish your teen years? Make a few notes here:

_____

_____

_____

A Christian must be aware of the consequences of sin—disqualification (verse 27). In the Olympic Games of Paul's day, a contestant who failed to meet basic training requirements and event rules could not participate in the race. In the same way, a self-absorbed young man disqualifies himself when he is unwilling to pay the price to learn and grow in the knowledge of God's rules—to discover the rules in the Bible. After you become a Christian, being ignorant of God's rules is never a valid excuse.

When Justin finished, Zack looked stunned and said, "Wow—I didn't realize that being a Christian was this serious!"

Justin then looked Zack in the eyes. "That's why I wanted to meet with you, Zack. In you I saw someone who wasn't wanting to play spiritual games. I saw someone who might be willing to accept the disciplines that should mark the life of every Christian. I see you're wanting to be more disciplined, and you want to understand your Bible better. But there's another discipline you'll need—Bible study's twin brother, prayer. These two disciplines—Bible study and prayer—are the two sides of the coin of Christian maturity.

"To get you started, I'm going to give you a Bible study on prayer. Before you started coming to youth group, I took the guys through a book called *A Young Man's Guide to Making Right Choices*.[1] In that book is a chapter on prayer that will help you better understand its importance. Let's pray that this study will help motivate you in the discipline of prayer."

Zack could hardly wait to get home and start discovering what the Bible says about prayer. Let's join him and find out what he learned.

God Is Available to You—24/7!

"Is that your cell phone ringing?" You hear people say this every day. It seems like everyone has a cell phone with country-wide coverage. There are very few places where you can't receive a cell phone signal.

In many ways, your prayer life is like a cell phone—you can pray to God anytime you want, anywhere you want, for as long as you want. But unlike a cell phone, prayer has no fees or roaming charges. You also never have to scroll through a directory to find God's number and contact information. And your communication with God requires no earpiece—it's hands-free. Plus you have a direct line to the God of the universe 24/7/365—24 hours a day, 7 days a week, 365 days per year. How's that for technology? Divine technology, that is.

It's clear throughout the Bible that God answers prayer. Then why don't we pray more often? Why aren't we more serious about the discipline of prayer?

10 Reasons We Don't Pray

With the act of prayer being as easy as bowing your head

and simply talking to God about what is going on in your life, you'd think that we'd pray a lot more than we do. Have you ever thought about why you don't pray more? I'm sure you have. And so have I—all the time, in fact! As I look at my own heart and life, I've discovered some reasons—and excuses—that we use for not praying.

1. *Worldliness*—Our world affects us more than we think. It exerts a constant pressure on us to live the same way the world lives…instead of living God's way. And besides, because we already have food, clothing, shelter, family, friends, and lots of fun things to do, we wrongly decide, "Why do I need to talk to God? I've got everything I need without wasting my time praying."

2. *Busyness*—Another reason we don't pray is because we don't take the time or make an effort to pray. Prayer isn't a priority for us, so we fill our time with other things we think are more important. We're so busy we don't even get around to planning the act of praying into our daily schedule.

3. *Foolishness*—Whenever we're consumed with what's foolish, trivial, and meaningless, we fail to pray. We begin to lose our ability to know the difference between what is good and what is not good. Between what is essential and what isn't. Between what is eternal and what is temporary. Everything becomes a "gray area" that doesn't require prayer. (Or so we think!)

4. *Distance*—We have no problem talking with friends. You can talk to your friends about video games for hours—and you do! But talk to someone outside your circle? Forget it. We are the same way when it comes to talking to God. When your relationship with God isn't a close one, you will find it hard to talk to Him. You won't know what to say, and you won't feel close to Him or comfortable in His presence.

5. *Ignorance*—We're clueless about how prayer works. And we don't understand how it helps or fits into our relationship with God and making right choices. The problem is we don't fully understand God's love for us and His power to make our lives better.

6. *Sinfulness*—We don't pray because we know we've done something wrong. In our hearts we know we need to talk to God about it, confess it, agree with Him that what we did was wrong. What can we do about our sins and failures? Make a choice to keep short accounts with God. Deal with any sin as it comes up—on the spot—at the exact moment that you slip up and fail.

7. *Faithlessness*—We don't really believe in the power of prayer. Sometimes that's because we don't know the many promises God has made to us about prayer. We don't know about His assurances of answered prayer. Therefore we assume prayer doesn't make a difference for us. So we don't pray.

8. *Pridefulness*—Prayer shows our dependence on God. When we fail to pray, in our pride we're saying that we don't have any needs—or worse, we're saying, "No thanks, God. I'll take care of this. I've got it. I'm good."

9. *Inexperience*—We don't pray because…we don't pray! And because we don't pray, we don't know how to pray…so we still don't pray! We're like a dog chasing after its tail, caught in a cycle that leads nowhere.

10. *Laziness*—This may be our chief obstacle to prayer. We simply can't or won't put out the effort to talk to God. Prayer is an act of the will. It's a choice. You have to want to do it, and choose to do it.

Look over the list of excuses for not praying and pick the top two that usually keep you from praying. What steps can you take to eliminate these excuses?

1. _____

_____

_____

2. _____

_____

_____

Promises About Prayer

Now it's your turn to discover what your Bible says about prayer. As you read each of these amazing promises and assurances about prayer, circle what is required of you, and then write out God's promise to you.

"Whatever you ask for in prayer, believe that you have received it" (Mark 11:24).

_____

_____

_____

"Call to me and I will answer you and tell you great and unsearchable things you do not know" (Jeremiah 33:3).

_____

_____

_____

"Let us then approach God's throne of grace with confidence, so that we may receive mercy and find grace to help us in our time of need" (Hebrews 4:16).

_____

_____

_____

_____

"Is anyone among you in trouble? Let them pray" (James 5:13).

_____

_____

_____

"If any of you lacks wisdom, you should ask God...and it will be given to you" (James 1:5).

_____

_____

_____

"Love your enemies and pray for those who persecute you" (Matthew 5:44).

_____

_____

_____

_____

"If we confess our sins, [God] is faithful and just and will forgive us our sins and purify us from all unrighteousness" (1 John 1:9).

_____

_____

_____

"Whatever you ask for in prayer believe that you have received it, and it will be yours" (Mark 11:24).

_____

_____

_____

"You do not have, because you do not ask God. When you ask, you do not receive, because you ask with wrong motives, that you may spend what you get on your pleasures" (James 4:2-3). What word of caution does God give for when you pray?

_____

_____

_____

Examples of Men Who Prayed

As you begin to use your Bible more and more, you will discover that it is filled with people who made the choice to pray about everything in life—who sharpened their weapon of prayer. See what you can learn about the difference prayer made in these people's lives, and what kinds of issues they talked over with God.

David—Read Psalm 32:1-5. What was the issue in David's life, and how did prayer make a difference?

_____

_____

_____

Abraham—Read Genesis 18:20-33 and 19:29. What was Abraham's concern, and what did he do about it? What was the result?

_____

_____

_____

Jesus—Read Luke 6:12-13. How long did Jesus pray, and what decision did He make afterward?

_____

_____

_____

Take time to write down the decisions you are facing these days, and then pick a time when you will pray about them—on a daily basis.

Decisions I need to pray about:

_____

_____

_____

Jesus—read Matthew 26:36-44. What takes place in these verses, and what was Jesus' intention according to verse 36?

_____

_____

_____

How is the seriousness of Jesus' situation described in verses 37-38?

_____

_____

_____

According to verse 39, what was Jesus' posture when He prayed?

_____

_____

_____

Jesus was praying about the fact He would soon die on the cross. How many times did He pray about doing God's will (verses 39-44)? And what desire was repeatedly expressed in the content of His prayers in verses 39, 42, and 44?

_____

_____

_____

After extended time in prayer, how did Jesus proceed
to fulfill God's plan that He die for sinners (see verses
45-46)?

_____

_____

_____

_____

_____

Paul—Read Philippians 4:6. What prompted Paul to
pray?

_____

_____

_____

List the types of prayer that Paul mentions in verse 6.

_____

_____

_____

What happens when we give all our anxieties over to
God in prayer, according to verse 7?

_____

_____

_____

_____

TAKING IT ALL IN

So do you want to use your secret weapon of prayer? Here are two simple principles that will move you forward and help you overcome the excuses for not praying:

First, head to bed a little earlier. Set a goal of getting up five minutes earlier in the morning so you have time to pray. Prayer takes at least a few minutes.

To make this happen, finish your homework the night before. Do all your pre-bed stuff, like washing your face and brushing your teeth. Then check your schedule for the next day and begin a to-do list for tomorrow. Put prayer at the top of the list. Set out your Bible and prayer notebook in the place where you plan to have your quiet time the next morning. You can even create your prayer list the night before so that you are ready to pray as soon as you wake up.

Then get to bed a little earlier so you can meet with God and start developing the habit of prayer and talking with your heavenly Father each morning.

Second, remember the principle "Something is better than nothing." Any prayer is better than no prayer. Some prayer is better than none. Start by making the choice to pray a few minutes each morning. Then graduate little by little to more time spent in prayer.

What Others Have Said About the Bible

The New Testament is the best book the world has ever known or will know.
CHARLES DICKENS, Author

4

One God, One Book, One Message

*All Scripture is God-breathed
and is useful for teaching,
rebuking, correcting and training in righteousness.*
2 TIMOTHY 3:16

Zack couldn't wait to get to Justin's office for their next session together. This feeling was definitely new for Zack! In the past he tried to avoid getting too excited about anything that might show some hint of interest on his part. That was the way cool teen guys were supposed to act, right? They were to always have a bored look on their face.

But Zack was changing. He could tell. He was genuinely excited about learning to understand his Bible, and the homework assignment on prayer had been awesome. He had never realized prayer was so important! He and Justin had met only a few times, but during each visit Zack learned a lot. So Zack was excited about what Justin had waiting for him on this next visit.

As Zack approached Justin's office, Justin was sitting at his desk looking at the material he wanted to go over with Zack. He heard Zack knock on the door, and before he could say, "Come in," the door burst open and Zack charged in with a big grin on his face.

"Boy, do I want to thank you for that lesson on prayer! It was eye-opening. I've even started praying each morning. I feel closer to God and have a new boldness about living for Him. Prayer has really given me confidence to live for Jesus, and I've noticed the help He gives me throughout the day as I talk to Him."

Justin was thrilled that Zack was excited about prayer because it is such a key part of studying the Bible. As they opened their meeting with prayer, Justin could sense a real difference in Zack. When they finished praying, Justin didn't waste any time getting started.

"Zack, before we get into the mechanics of Bible study, there's just one more preliminary lesson we need to cover. It's about the big picture of God's Word. The Bible is made up of sixty-six different books written by about forty authors. The Old Testament was originally written in Hebrew and the New Testament in Greek, and many people don't understand how the two testaments work together.

"Some people assume the New Testament is all they need, and that the Old Testament is outdated. But that's not correct. This week, we'll learn how the Old and New Testaments fit together. We're going to do a little survey of the one book about the one and only God with one message."

Justin then gave Zack a worksheet and a pen and said, "Take this worksheet and use your Bible's table of contents to complete it. We'll go over it next week."

On the next few pages, you'll find the same information that Justin gave to Zack. Follow along, and write your answers in the blanks provided.

The Old Testament

The Old Testament is a record of God's dealing with His "chosen people," or the nation of Israel. Back in ancient times, people did not follow God, and they worshiped all sorts of idols. Therefore God founded the Hebrew nation to establish the idea that there is only one true living God. His desire was for the Jewish people to make Him known to the other nations.

The first five books of the Old Testament were written about 1450 BC by Moses. These are called the five books of Moses, or the Pentateuch (meaning "five scrolls or writings"). In Judaism, they are called the Torah, meaning "the law." List these five books of the Bible below in the order you find them in your Bible's table of contents.

1. _____ is the book of beginnings (creation, man, sin, redemption, God's nation).

2. _____ shows God delivering His people from Egypt.

3. _____ details priestly laws on holiness and worship through sacrifices and purification.

4. _____ explains how God's people continually disobeyed Him and wandered in the wilderness for 40 years.

5. _____ records Moses teaching a new generation of people and preparing them to enter the Promised Land.

The next 12 books of the Bible are referred to as the historical books. They were written about 1100–600 BC. These books describe God's dealings with His chosen people after they entered the Promised Land. Using your Bible's table of contents, list these historical books in order.

1. _____ highlights the conquest of the Promised Land.

2. _____ portrays the people's disobedience and God's deliverance through His appointed judges.

3. _____ is a story of the redemption of an outcast who joined the family line of Messiah.

4. _____ describes Israel's transition from 12 independent tribes into a kingdom.

5. _____ details the unification of the 12 tribes of Israel.

6. _____ records the division of Israel into two nations.

7. _____ shows the dispersion of the northern and southern kingdoms of Israel.

8. _____ is a written record of Israel's spiritual history.

9. _____ is a written record of Israel's spiritual heritage.

10. _____ contains information about
the Jews' return from captivity.

11. _____ presents an account of the
rebuilding of the wall around Jerusalem.

12. _____ shows how God preserved
Queen Esther and saved the Jews from annihilation.

The next five books of the Old Testament are known as the poetical books. They include Hebrew poems and songs that describe God's greatness and His dealings with mankind. List these books in order below, and notice what each book is about.

1. _____ shines a spotlight on the
suffering and loyal trust of a man who loved God.

2. _____ is a collection of 150 songs
of praise and instruction on worship.

3. _____ logs 31 chapters of God's
practical wisdom for successful living.

4. _____ laments the emptiness of
earthly life without God.

5. _____ looks at the marriage
relationship between a man and a woman as a portrait
of God's love for His people.

The next five books in the Bible are called the major prophets. This is not because these prophets are greater in their importance, but because the books they wrote were longer. These books were written from about 750–550 BC. List them below and notice what each book is about.

1. _____ tells of salvation through the coming Messiah.

2. _____ proclaims God's judgment of Israel.

3. _____ documents a prophet's lament about the fall of Jerusalem.

4. _____ declares the glory of the Lord.

5. _____ proclaims the sovereignty of God.

The last 12 books of the Old Testament are called the minor prophets. That's because the books are generally shorter than the books known as the major prophets. These books were written from about 800–400 BC. List them in the order they appear in your Bible, and again notice what each one is about.

1. _____ describes Israel's unfaithfulness to God.

2. _____ talks about the day of the Lord.

3. _____ records the judgment of Israel's northern kingdom.

4._____ speaks of the righteous judgment of Edom.

5._____ proclaims God's grace to all people.

6._____ documents the judgment of Israel's southern kingdom.

7._____ warns of Nineveh's destruction unless the people turn to God.

8._____ talks about trusting God, who is sovereign.

9._____ declares the "great day of the Lord."

10._____ tells about rebuilding the temple.

11._____ proclaims God's deliverance through Jesus the Messiah.

12._____ is a book in which legalism is rebuked.

All together, there are 39 books in the Old Testament. These, along with the 27 books in the New Testament, bring us to a total of 66 books in the Bible. You will find it extremely helpful to memorize the order in which these books appear.

The New Testament

One primary purpose of the Old Testament was to let the people of the world realize their need for a Savior from their sins. The law of Moses was to serve as a "tutor" to point people toward Christ and salvation. In the New Testament we read about Christ's arrival on earth—we read about His life, His death, and His resurrection, which makes it possible for God to rescue us from our sins. Then we read God's instructions for Christian living as well as His plans for the future.

The first five books of the New Testament are the historical books. As you did with the Old Testament, use the table of contents in your Bible to fill in the blanks for these five historical books of the New Testament.

1. _____ Here you will find the life of Christ written especially for the Jewish people, revealing Jesus Christ as their long-awaited Messiah and King.

2. _____ This book about the life of Christ reveals Jesus as the obedient servant of God and emphasizes His activities.

3. _____ Here the life of Christ reveals Jesus as the perfect man, emphasizing His humanity.

4. _____ In this book, we see Christ revealed as the Son of God, stressing His deity.

5. _____ This historical book charts the beginning and spread of the Christian church. Because this book repeatedly mentions the Holy Spirit, it is sometimes called the Acts of the Holy Spirit.

Just a note: The first four books in the New Testament are referred to as the the four Gospels. Why four? They were written by four different biographers who recorded Jesus' life from four different perspectives: Jesus as king, as servant, as man, and as God.

The Gospel of John gives two reasons that John was careful to record the details about the life of Jesus. Read them in John 20:30-31, and list the two reasons found in verse 31:

1. _____

_____

2. _____

_____

The next 21 books are letters, which are also referred to as the epistles. They were written to individuals, to churches, or to all believers in general. These letters deal with every aspect of the Christian faith and your responsibilities as a believer in Christ. List them below in the order you find them in your Bible. And don't forget to notice the theme of each book.

Group 1 — The letters of the apostle Paul written to churches or individuals

1. _____ The righteousness of God

2. _____ Christian conduct

3. _____ Paul's defense of his apostleship

4. _____ Freedom in Christ

5. _____ Blessings in Christ

6. _____ The joy-filled life

7. _____ The supremacy of Christ

8. _____ Concern for the church

9. _____ Living in hope

10. _____ Instructions for a young disciple

11. _____ A charge to faithful ministry

12. _____ A manual of conduct

13. _____ A request for forgiveness

Group 2—General letters written to groups of Jews scattered across the Roman world

1. _____ The superiority of Christ

2. _____ Genuine faith

3. _____ Responding to suffering

4. _____ Warning against false teachers

5. _____ Fellowship with God

6. _____ Christian discernment

7. _____ Christian hospitality

8. _____ Contending for the faith

The last book of the New Testament is a book of prophecy. It tells of future events including the return, reign, and glory of the Lord Jesus Christ, and the future state of believers and unbelievers. It is called _____ .

The Unity of the Old and New Testaments

The best way to get a good sense for the unity of the Bible as a whole is to see the way the New Testament looks at the Old Testament.

First, let's consider authorship. According to Hebrews 1:1-2, who spoke the content that is found in both the Old and New Testaments? Read the verses below, then write your answer.

> In the past God spoke to our ancestors through the prophets at many times and in various ways [Old Testament], but in these last days he has spoken to us by his Son, whom he appointed heir of all things, and through whom also he made the universe [New Testament].

_____

_____

Second, notice there is one plan of redemption. Read 2 Timothy 3:14-15 and notice how the Old Testament pointed Timothy to salvation:

> As for you [Timothy], continue in what you have learned and have become convinced of, because you know those from whom you learned it, and

> how from infancy you have known the Holy
> Scriptures [the Old Testament], which are able
> to make you wise for salvation through faith in
> Christ Jesus.

Now read Romans 4:1-9 in your Bible. There the apostle Paul says that both Abraham and David were justified by faith. Again you see one plan of redemption—faith alone—for salvation.

Third, Jesus is at the center of it all. All through the Old Testament, we see statements that look ahead to the coming Messiah who would rescue people from their sins. Even as early as Genesis 3:15, in the first book of the Bible, we find a mention of Christ. We are also told that Christ had a part in making the universe—Hebrews 1:2 says that God "has spoken to us by his Son...through whom also he made the universe."

Read Colossians 1:16. What does it say about the creation of the world? Write the answer below.

> In him all things were created: things in heaven
> and on earth, visible and invisible, whether thrones
> or powers or rulers or authorities; all things have
> been created through him and for him.

_____

_____

Christ appeared multiple times throughout the Old Testament. These appearances are called *theophanies*, or appearances by God. Christ Himself is referred to as "the radiance of God's glory" (Hebrews 1:3). How is Christ described in Genesis 16:7?

_____

_____

"The angel of the LORD" in Genesis 16:7 is mentioned again in verse 10. There we see that He possesses the kind of authority that belongs to God alone, as seen in His ability to care for the descendants of Hagar and her son, Ishmael.

Fourth, we see the unity of the Old and New Testaments in the national redemption of Israel. The fact the people of Israel still exist today is a mighty proof of God's power. He has preserved them through the ages. And in 1 Corinthians 10:1-11, Paul talks about how God used the Old Testament nation of Israel to teach many truths to New Testament believers. In Romans chapters 9–11, Paul explains that God is not finished with Israel. Israel as a nation has a place in God's future plans. That is confirmed for us in the book of Revelation.

The Contrasts Between the Old and New Testaments

In addition to the unity we see between the Old and New Testaments, there are also some points of contrast. We will consider a few of them here.

First, God revealed Himself in different ways in each testament. In the Old Testament, the Holy Spirit was said to "come upon a person" once in a great while for unusual times of service to God. But in the New Testament, we read that the Holy Spirit lives in all believers (Ephesians 1:13-14).

Second, the Old Testament focused on God's law while the New Testament focuses on God's grace. A key purpose of the law was to show people they were sinners in need of a Savior, and God's grace makes salvation from sin a free gift through faith in Jesus Christ.

Third, the Old Testament shows God involved in different covenant relationships with Noah, Abraham, the nation of

Israel, and King David. These comprise the old covenants. In the New Testament, Jesus spoke of believers being part of a new covenant—a new covenant of the heart.

When we look at the points of unity and contrast, we get a much better idea of how the Old and New Testaments work together. We see how God has continued to work in people's lives through the ages, and how He has revealed more and more about that work as time goes on.

There are some people who call this "progressive revelation." What does that mean? Think of it this way: As you read through your Bible, picture yourself driving down a highway and looking at the road signs. Each road sign will give you a little bit of information about what lies ahead. As you pass more and more signs, you get a more complete picture of everything that is ahead of you. In the same way, as you make your way through the Bible, you are able to get a more and more complete picture of what God wants you to know.

So in the Old Testament, we see how God works in people's lives, and we see His plan for the future unfolding. Then in the New Testament we see a key part of His plan revealed in the coming of Jesus Christ to earth. After that we learn how we as Christians are to live out our salvation. All of this makes the Bible an incredible book!

TAKING IT ALL IN

So far, we have learned that the Bible is a special book. It is the revealed Word and will of God. It tells us about God and His desire for our lives.

Do you want to know God's will? Then you must read the Bible. But a word of caution: Know that as you read and study the Bible, God will demand a response. He will expect you to grow in your obedience, faith, and love for Him and His Word.

The good news about all this is God doesn't expect you to do this on your own. He will help you at each and every step along the way. Jesus offers this encouragement:

> Come to me, all you who are weary and burdened, and I will give you rest. Take my yoke upon you and learn from me, for I am gentle and humble in heart, and you will find rest for your souls. For my yoke is easy and my burden is light (Matthew 11:28-30).

What Others Said About the Bible

Sin will keep you from the Bible, or the Bible will keep you from sin.

DWIGHT L. MOODY
19th-Century Evangelist

5

A Book of Great Value

*The law from your mouth is more precious to me
than thousands of pieces of silver and gold.*

PSALM 119:72

With his worksheet in hand, Zack greeted Pastor Justin, sat down, and proudly presented his homework. Justin grinned and said, "Pretty easy assignment, wasn't it?"

Zack nodded in agreement, but added, "I found out I didn't know much about the Old Testament, and this exercise helped put some things in place for me. It's nice to get the big picture of what God was doing over those thousands of years. And to see it all come together in the New Testament. God is incredible!"

And then Zack thought to himself, *That's an understatement if I ever heard one!*

"So, Zack, it looks like you and I are still on the same page when it comes to appreciating the Bible. Let's take our study one step further. We've already answered the 'What is the Bible?' question. Now it's time to consider the next question: 'Why is this book so special?'

"To get you started," Justin continued, "let's look at the Bible as an archaeologist would look at a rare and ancient artifact. He would be carful to analyze it, not wanting to miss any important clues as to its origin and information.

"Or maybe you could imagine yourself as a master spy," Justin said. "You would look at the Bible as if it were a top-secret journal that you've just retrieved from behind enemy lines. You would treat it with great interest and the utmost care because you know it contains valuable material that is vital to national security.

"Either way, as an archaeologist or a master spy, you must have a starting point. Let's start at the beginning."

The Origins of the Bible

The Bible didn't just miraculously appear one day out of nowhere. Nor was the Bible's revelation attributed to the wisdom or holiness of one person or even a handful of men. The Bible, in contrast to all other religious writings, was written over a period of 1500 years, beginning with the time of the great Pharaohs of Egypt around 1400 BC, and ending with the last book of the Bible, Revelation, which was completed around AD 95 while the world was dominated by the mighty Roman Empire. The majority of the Bible was written in two languages—Hebrew and Greek, and its 66 books have been attributed to the pens of more than 40 different authors.

In the 2000-plus years since the Bible was written, it has been passed down through the centuries and translated into many of the world's languages. This has led to a question often asked by skeptics: How can we be sure the Bible's message hasn't been altered by the carelessness or the evil intent of men? And what about the possibility of incorrect translation work on account of cultural and linguistic barriers? Isn't there a danger that the Bible's message would have changed?

This might be true of other written works, but it is not the case with the Bible. Its message is the same as back when it was penned. We have been able to compare the earliest copies of the Bible with the modern copies, and they are exactly the same. Yet the skeptics continue to drill, "How can this be?" This is one of the reasons we study the Bible. When we consider that God Himself wrote the Bible through human instruments, that His Word is perfect, and that those who copied Bible manuscripts through the ages were extremely careful to maintain accuracy, we can better understand how it is that the Bible of today is the same Bible that was originally written. God is able to preserve the truth that has been passed down in His Word.

Setting the Record Straight

The Bible is an amazing book. There is a difference between it and all other books, even other religious books. Their authors claim to be spokesmen for their deity, either the Christian God or another god. Yet none of these authors can claim that God Himself wrote their books.

That is the unique claim of the Bible. God used each writer's personality, language, background, vocabulary, and historical knowledge in the course of guiding them along as they wrote the Bible. He had a message He wanted to communicate to all people, and He worked everything out so His message would be communicated accurately. Though people were used to write the Bible, it is actually the writings of God Himself. That's why we can call the Bible God's Word.

Looking at God's Claim

The Old Testament alone asserts more than 2000 times that it is the Word of God. The phrase "the word of God" also occurs more than 40 times in the New Testament. Here are a few examples—circle each time you find "word of God" used.

1. Jesus affirmed the Old Testament as the Word of God when He confronted the religious leaders of His day:

> You nullify the word of God by your tradition that you have handed down (Mark 7:13).

2. Jesus preached it:

> One day as Jesus was standing by the Lake of Gennesaret, the people were crowding around him and listening to the word of God (Luke 5:1).

3. Paul and his missionary team preached it:

> When they arrived at Salamis, they proclaimed the word of God in the Jewish synagogues (Acts 13:5).

4. Paul described the Bible as a part of the Christian's spiritual armor:

> Take the helmet of salvation and the sword of the Spirit, which is the word of God (Ephesians 6:17).

Looking at the Process

So you get the idea now: The Bible is God's Word as communicated through the Holy Spirit to men. Like every book that's ever been written, the Bible had a publishing process. To ensure the purity of His message, God took the Bible through His protective publishing process, which involves five features.

1. *Revelation*—This means to disclose information that might not have been known or realized before. As the Bible says in John 4:24, "God is spirit." We cannot see Him. So God took the initiative and revealed Himself to us so we would know who He is. How does the following verse describe the process God used to reveal Himself?

Long ago God spoke many times and in many ways to our ancestors through the prophets. And now in these final days, he has spoken to us through his Son (Hebrews 1:1-2 NLT).

_____

_____

_____

2. *Inspiration*—The revelation of God was captured in the writing of the Bible by means of inspiration, or an influence. *Inspiration* has more to do with the process by which God revealed Himself than the revelation itself. How does this verse claim we received the Bible?

All Scripture is given by inspiration of God (2 Timothy 3:16 NKJV).

_____

_____

_____

Look at 2 Timothy 3:16 again, but this time in the NIV Bible (see below). How does the NIV Bible translate the word "inspiration"?

All Scripture is God-breathed.

_____

_____

_____

In 2 Peter 1:20-21, how does Peter explain the process of inspiration, or being "God-breathed," and how God passed information along to man?

> Above all, you must understand that no prophecy of Scripture came about by the prophet's own interpretation of things. For prophecy never had its origin in the human will, but prophets, though human, spoke from God as they were carried along by the Holy Spirit.

Note: Through the process of inspiration, the Word of God was protected from human error in its original record by the ministry of the Holy Spirit.

3. *Canonicity*—This word is the answer to the question, "How do we know if the authentic sacred writings actually made it into what we now know as the Bible?" This is where the word *canon* comes in. No, this is not a weapon. *Canon* is used to describe the process of validating the Bible. It refers to a measuring rod or standard for determining exactly which writings were to be included in God's Word. If a certain manuscript didn't meet the standard, it was left out of the Bible.

Certain principles were used to determine which books should be included in the Bible. By the time of Christ, all of the Old Testament had been written and had met the accepted standard by Jewish scholars. As different books of the New Testament were written and circulated, many were already being seen as authentic. As the years went on, groups of Christian scholars got together to determine which writings belonged in the Bible. After much discussion, the early leaders of the church came to agree on which books were declared inspired by God and to be included in the New Testament.

What does the apostle Peter say about Paul's writings that affirmed Peter's belief that Paul's writings were from God? (Notice the italicized words.)

Bear in mind that our Lord's patience means salvation, just as our dear brother Paul also wrote you with the wisdom that God gave him. He writes the same way in all his letters, speaking in them of these matters. His letters contain some things that are hard to understand, which ignorant and unstable people distort, *as they do the other Scriptures*, to their own destruction (2 Peter 3:15-16).

_____

_____

_____

4. *Preservation*—This answers the question, "How can we be sure that the revealed and inspired Word of God, which was recognized as authentic by the early church, has been handed down to us today without any loss of material or meaning?"

Let's see the promise God made concerning His Word:

The grass withers and the flowers fall, but the word of our God endures forever (Isaiah 40:8).

_____

_____

_____

What is another promise God makes concerning the consistency of His Word?

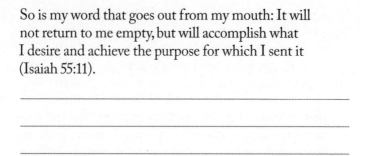

So is my word that goes out from my mouth: It will
not return to me empty, but will accomplish what
I desire and achieve the purpose for which I sent it
(Isaiah 55:11).

_____

_____

_____

5. *Transmission*—This deals with the translation of the Bible into different languages. The Bible was originally written in Hebrew and Aramaic in the Old Testament, and Greek in the New Testament. Until the arrival of the printing press in AD 1450 the Bible was copied by hand, which increased the possibility that errors could creep into it. However, those who did this copying had great reverence for the Bible and were very careful in their work. That's why, when we compare early copies of the Bible with those from today, they are almost exactly alike.

New Testament scholars believe today's Bibles have preserved about 99.99 percent of the original text. Therefore, we can rest assured that our translations today are indeed worthy of the title of the Word of God.

Are You Looking for More?

Isn't it great to know you have a 99.99 percent chance of reading the exact words that the original authors of the Bible wrote down? But is this everything? Is there anything else God wants to communicate to us? Are there any new truths He wants to pass on? There are some people who believe the answer is yes.

If this is the case, should we be looking for new books to add to the Bible? Or is it possible there is a lost book or two out there floating around somewhere?

When it comes to answering such questions, it's important

to keep in mind the following warnings from the Bible. Note what they say about adding or deleting anything from God's Word:

> Do not add to what I command you and do not subtract from it, but keep the commands of the Lord your God that I give you (Deuteronomy 4:2).

> See that you do all I command you; do not add to it or take away from it (Deuteronomy 12:32).

> Do not add to his words, or he will rebuke you and prove you a liar (Proverbs 30:6).

Now look at perhaps the most compelling verses on God's commands that nothing is to be added to or taken away from the Scriptures:

> I warn everyone who hears the words of the prophecy of this scroll: If anyone adds anything to them, God

will add to that person the plagues described in this scroll. And if anyone takes words away from this scroll of prophecy, God will take away from that person any share in the tree of life and in the Holy City, which are described in this scroll (Revelation 22:18-19).

_____

_____

_____

How Valuable Is the Bible?

Do you remember how this chapter began? Justin spoke to Zack about the value of the Bible. When we speak of value, we are not talking about monetary value. Rather, we are talking about the Bible's spiritual value. Read what the psalmist said about the value of the Bible:

> The law from your mouth is more precious to me
> than thousands of pieces of silver and gold (Psalm
> 119:72).

What makes the Bible so valuable? Look at the following verses and state your answers. (If you have trouble figuring out the answers, here are your options: salvation, direction, truth, obedience, victory, growth.)

1. The Bible is your source of _____

> Sanctify them by the truth; your word is truth (John
> 17:17).

2. The Bible is your source of _____

> [Jesus] replied, 'Blessed rather are those who hear
> the word of God and obey it (Luke 11:28).

3. The Bible is your source of spiritual

_____

> Everyone born of God overcomes the world. This is the victory that has overcome the world, even our faith (1 John 5:4).

4. The Bible is your source of spiritual

_____

> Like newborn babies, crave pure spiritual milk, so that by it you may grow up in your salvation (1 Peter 2:2).

5. The Bible is your source of _____

> I am not ashamed of the gospel, because it is the power of God that brings salvation to everyone who believes: first to the Jew, then to the Gentile (Romans 1:16).

6. The Bible is your source of _____

> Your word is a lamp for my feet, a light on my path (Psalm 119:105).

TAKING IT ALL IN

I'm sure you have heard of rare comic books being sold at auctions for incredibly high prices. But are they truly worth that much? Does a fiction or fantasy tale really have the kind of value that is found in the Bible? Tragically, many Christians don't show much interest in the Bible. They don't value it as they should.

How much do you value your Bible? Are your interests more along the lines of comic book purchases? Or is your appreciation for the Bible like that of a man in one of Jesus' parables? This man found a hidden treasure in a field, and sold all that he had to buy and claim this one treasure (Matthew 13:44). What was this "hidden treasure" the man wanted so much? According to the parable, it was the kingdom of heaven. In other words, the things of God are worth far more than the things of this world.

This may be a heavy question to place on your shoulders, but you are now entering the age when you are capable of making important choices and decisions. And here's one such decision: Will you choose to pick up your Bible, read it, learn how to study it, and most importantly, live it? Or will you choose to view the Bible as a book you can't understand and can live without, and therefore ignore it? Which choice will you make?

God is not asking you to sell everything or even anything. He is only asking you to give Him your life and spend time getting to know Him and His plan for your life—which is made possible by reading and studying His Word.

Again, which choice will you make?

Jim Elliot, a missionary who was martyred in his late twenties, said it well:

> He is no fool who gives what he cannot keep
> to gain what he cannot lose.

The Bible contains the words of life, but you must open it to find out what they are!

What Others Said About the Bible

The Bible is worth all the other books which have ever been printed.

PATRICK HENRY
First Governor of Virginia; famous for saying,
"Give me liberty or give me death."

6

What Do You See?

*My son, if you accept my words and store up
my commands within you, turning your ear to
wisdom and applying your heart to understanding—
indeed, if you call out for insight and cry aloud
for understanding, and if you look for it as for silver
and search for it as for hidden treasure,
then you will understand the fear of the LORD
and find the knowledge of God.*

PROVERBS 2:1-5

As Zack entered Pastor Justin's office to continue their ongoing quest to understand the Bible, Justin said, "Hey, Zack, stop right there! Turn around—I want to take you out to the church parking lot." With a quizzical expression on his face, Zack complied, turned around, and walked with Justin out to the parking lot.

They stopped in the middle of the lot, and Zack still couldn't figure out what Justin had in mind. After a brief lull, Justin asked, "What do you see, Zack?"

"What do you mean?" Zack replied.

Justin made a sweeping gesture with his arms and said, "Look around and tell me—what do you see?"

"Er...ah...well, I see parked cars, asphalt, the church buildings, and cars passing by on the street in front of the church," said Zack.

"Can you be more specific?" said Justin.

Noticing Zack's questioning glance, Justin explained: "What are the makes, models, and colors of the cars? How would you describe the church building? What is the weather like?"

Before Zack could answer, Justin added, "This is a first and important step in understanding the Bible—looking beyond the surface and getting specific. It's called *observation*. The purpose of observation is to answer the questions, "What does it say?" and "What do I see?"

Learning to Look

Justin caught Zack off guard. He made Zack realize he wasn't looking very closely at what he was seeing. That's because Zack wasn't paying close attention to the specifics.

That's true for a lot of people. In fact, that's the problem the police run into when they ask witnesses what happened at the scene of a crime or an accident. The witnesses might have seen what happened, but they weren't observing closely the details of what happened. So when the police interview the witnesses, they often end up with different accounts of the same event.

What kind of observer are you? Being good at observation requires training. In the case of the police, FBI, or CIA, this means looking for what is different, unusual, abnormal, or out of place. When it comes to the Bible, this involves doing more than just reading the words. It requires taking the time to understand what is being said.

If you want to get more out of your Bible, then it's important to become a good observer. To start you out, there are basically two types of observation:

Supernatural observation: This type of observation can only be possessed by a Christian. As we have already learned, "the person without the Spirit" cannot understand the things of God (1 Corinthians 2:14-15). A person without God cannot understand the things of God. Hopefully, you are a believer in Christ and already have the benefit of God's gift of spiritual insight through the Holy Spirit.

Natural observation: Unlike supernatural observation, natural observation can be learned, developed, and improved. Just as a police officer is trained in how and what to observe, you can learn what to look for as you read your Bible. So let's start with the simple process of learning how to read your Bible.

How to Read Your Bible

When it comes to good observation, we're not talking about the simple mechanics of reading the words themselves; rather, we're talking about reading for understanding. Here are some quick tips to get you started in increasing your understanding of the Bible as you read it.

1. *Choose a translation that you can understand.* We haven't discussed translations of the Bible yet, but there are many good modern translations that you can use without having to stumble over difficult terms or archaic language.

2. *Don't try to see how fast you can read your Bible.* Read at your normal rate or even slower. Don't read just to see how fast you can turn the pages or finish. Read so that you remember what's on the page. Read to have your life changed. Read for wisdom and encouragement. Read for greater understanding. Read so that tomorrow or maybe even a year from now, you'll remember what you read today. Be a thoughtful reader, and not just a skimmer.

3. *Read with a pen or pencil in hand.* Underline passages or words that stand out to you. If you don't understand something, go ahead and put a question mark beside it so you can research it later. Write an exclamation point in the margin for something that excites you, or a star next to verses you want to remember or read again. If you are nervous about marking your Bible, don't be. It's not the physical ink and paper that's sacred, but rather, God's message itself. God wants you to understand your Bible well, so go ahead and mark it! Underline or circle key words or phrases. Make notes in the margins. All your interaction with a pen or pencil will help you to better grasp God's message to you.

Great Bible scholars, teachers, writers, and pastors like C.H. Spurgeon, Dwight L. Moody, C.I. Scofield, and C.S. Lewis made notes in their Bibles. It was part of how they got to know the Bible so well. Who knows? Maybe you will be the next Dwight L. Moody!

4. *Always read Bible verses with the surrounding passages in mind.* Keep in mind what happened in the section before the passage you are currently reading. In other words, get the big picture. If you have a study Bible, read the explanatory notes and comments that are in the margins or at the bottom of the page. If the book of the Bible you are reading has an introduction, read what it says. Knowing more about the big picture and what's happening will clue you in to what the author is thinking and wants you to know as a result of your reading.

5. *Check a dictionary for words you don't understand.* Or use your cell phone or computer to check out the words you're unsure of. This will build your vocabulary and help you better understand what you are reading.

6. *Stop at the end of each paragraph and figure out the main idea.* It takes only a few seconds to ask yourself, "What was this paragraph about?" Then as you string the paragraphs together and

determine what each one is about, you'll get a better sense for the main message of the passage you are reading.

The Act of Observation

Observation is the act and practice of noticing, and then noting those facts or events either mentally or on paper. What's involved in observation?

Observation requires concentration. You cannot watch TV and read your Bible at the same time without something getting lost in the process. That's why you need to set aside a quiet time for your Bible reading. Most of your day will be spent with people at your school, your family, and at various activities. You'll be bombarded all day long with different sights and sounds. But don't let those things crowd out your time with God. Set aside time to be alone with Him and His Word before you step out into your day. Take time to focus and concentrate on what God says to you as you read His Word.

Observation requires you ask the right questions. A journalist is someone who gathers facts and information to write news reports or newspaper articles. If you were to enroll in a journalism class at school, your teacher would probably send you "into the field" to report on an event at school or in the local area. As you do the research necessary to create your report, you would ask the following kinds of WH questions: Who? Where? When? What?

Using the WH questions, read Mark 1:29-31 in your Bible and practice observing:

Question #1: Who?

Who are the people in this paragraph? Note them all.

_____

_____

What is said about these people?

_____

_____

_____

Question #2: Where?

Where is this taking place? Note all descriptive information.

_____

_____

_____

What are the places mentioned?

_____

_____

_____

Question #3: When?

When is this taking place? Note all references to time.

_____

_____

_____

What time is it? Note references to time, time of day, or time in history.

_____

_____

_____

Question #4: What?

What is taking place in this paragraph?

_____

_____

_____

What is the point of this paragraph? Why do you think God wanted this information in the Bible and preserved for all time?

_____

_____

_____

Here are some examples on how to answer this question:

Is it a miracle?	What is happening?
Is it a parable?	What is its point?
Is it an argument?	How is it progressing?
Is it a sermon?	What's the message of the sermon?

Now that you're getting the idea, go ahead and try the WH questions on another Bible passage. Read Mark 1:32-35, and answer the following:

Who?

_____

_____

_____

What?

_____

_____

_____

Where?

_____

_____

_____

When?

_____

_____

_____

Why Ask Questions?

Are you thinking it doesn't seem to make sense to ask so many questions as you read the Bible? That it feels like all you are doing is talking to yourself? At first glance, it might seem a waste of time to ask what appear to be such obvious questions. But after you have done this for a while, you will discover that you are learning a lot. You will remember what the Bible says, which will make it easier for you to live it out in your life.

The main purpose of asking questions is to make you think more seriously and intelligently about the meaning and significance of the words, phrases, clauses, sentences, paragraphs, chapters, and books of the Bible. You get to ask questions of an author who lived thousands of years ago so you can determine what the author was trying to say to his readers, and what that means for you today.

For example, let's look at James 3:6. The book of James is believed to be the earliest of the New Testament books written. And James 3:6 happens to be an interesting verse:

> The tongue also is a fire, a world of evil among the
> parts of the body. It corrupts the whole body, sets
> the whole course of one's life on fire, and is itself
> set on fire by hell.

Now, what are some questions you could ask James, the author, about his statement, "The tongue also is a fire"? Ask them, and answer as many as you can:

"James, is this a literal statement? Are you saying the tongue is literally fire?"

"Are you speaking of the tongue as fire in a figurative sense, like a metaphor?" (Metaphors draw a comparison and sometimes use the word *like*—the tongue is *like* fire.)

"How could a person's tongue have the same effect
as a raging fire?"

You can probably think of a few kids at school who use
their tongues like weapons of destruction. Through the
words they speak, they hurt other people, put them
down, or make others look bad. What would be a good
application for you from James 3:6?

Looking for the Right Things

Let's go back to your assignment as a reporter. When it
comes to observation, you don't want to stop with just the WH
questions. As reporter at an event, you must look for additional
information. For example, do all the people who are witness-
ing the event describe it the same way? Are certain statements
repeated again and again? When you read the Bible, you want to
watch for that as well—things that are repeated may have special significance.

So what do you want to watch for?

1. *Look for terms, not words.* "What's the difference?" you ask.
Words can have many meanings. For example, consider the
word *trunk.* It can mean several different things. Write as many

of those meanings as you can think of. I've started by giving you one example:

Tree trunk

_____

_____

_____

What are some different ways the word *coast* could be used?

_____

_____

_____

Now we're ready to find out what a *term* is. Unlike a word, a term has only one meaning because it is part of a group of words. In the sentence "The oak tree has an enormous trunk," the term *trunk* has only one meaning. The trunk is the base that supports the oak tree. So as you look at a sentence or paragraph in the Bible, you are looking for a single meaning for each word that appears. Watching for this single meaning will help make the Bible clearer to you.

2. *Look for structure.* The basic structural unit of most writing is a paragraph, which should contain a complete thought. Let's say an author is writing about the variety of fish in the ocean. He won't normally describe sea turtles in the same paragraph with swordfish. So when an author switches paragraphs, he is usually switching subjects—in this case, from sea turtles to swordfish.

Read Mark 1:29-34, and observe what happens as you go from one paragraph to the next.

What is the subject of the paragraph in Mark 1:29-31?

_____

_____

_____

What is the subject of the paragraph in Mark 1:32-34?

_____

_____

_____

There are other things you can look for in a paragraph or a section. For example:

Things that are emphasized—Scan quickly through these two chapters in the New Testament and write your answers:

In a word or two, what is emphasized in 1 Corinthians 13?

_____

In a word or two, what is emphasized in Hebrews 11?

_____

Things that are repeated—As you discovered above, love is repeatedly mentioned in 1 Corinthians 13, and faith is repeatedly mentioned in Hebrews 11.

Scan Galatians 5. What word do you see repeated?

_____

Scan Psalm 119. Notice that nearly every verse in this psalm uses a term for the Word of God. In a few words, what is the repeated emphasis made by the writer of this psalm?

_____

_____

_____

_____

Things that are related to each other—Watch for things that are connected in some way, or relate to one another.

Cause and effect. Read Matthew 23:37-38 (NKJV). Jesus wanted the people of Jerusalem to accept Him.

How did the people receive Him? (Notice the word "but.")

_____

_____

What was the result, according to verse 38?

_____

_____

Question and answer. Read Romans 3:1-7.

What question is asked in verse 1?

_____

_____

What answer is given in verse 2?

_____

_____

What questions are asked in verse 3?

_____

_____

What answer is given in verse 4?

_____

_____

3. *Look for types of literary form.* There are different types of literature or writing. As you read the Bible, it is helpful to know what kind of literary form you are reading.

Prose—If the material you are reading is a story, it is called prose. Mark 1:29 and the following verses are prose. What is the story about?

_____

_____

_____

Discourse—If the material is made up of teaching, it is called a discourse. A discourse is a formal presentation or discussion, like what Moses did throughout the book of Deuteronomy. Briefly scan Deuteronomy chapter 5. What was Moses' subject here?

_____

The apostle Paul was a great teacher. Scan through Romans chapter 4. What subject is Paul covering here?

_____

_____

Poetry—Much of the poetry in the Bible is found in the books of Psalms, Proverbs, and the Song of Solomon.

Look at the book of Proverbs. How many chapters are there in Proverbs? _____

Many Bible teachers suggest you read one chapter of Proverbs on the day coinciding with that day of the month. For example, if today is the sixth day of the month, then you would read Proverbs chapter 6.

Look at the book of Psalms. How many chapters are in this book? _____

The chapters in the book of Psalms were written by a number of people. According to the chapters listed below, who were some of these writers? Who wrote…

Psalm 8—_____

Psalm 4—_____

Psalm 90—_____

Song of Solomon is a love story. According to chapter 1, Solomon and a young girl called the Shulammite are the two main characters in this poetic story.

Parables—The sections of the Bible that use stories to convey a certain meaning or illustrate a specific truth are called parables. Jesus often spoke in parables. Scan Matthew 13 and jot down a topic or two Jesus illustrates through the use of a parable.

_____

_____

_____

Prophecy—The sections of the Bible that deal with the last days and predict imminent disaster are the books of Daniel and Revelation. Read Revelation 21:1-2. What is it describing?

_____

_____

_____

Now for an exercise! Using what you've learned about observation, read Mark 1:35-39. Not every WH question can be answered in this passage, but I have included them here so you can see the value of having them available anytime you observe a passage.

Who?

_____

_____

_____

What?

_____

_____

_____

Where?

_____

_____

_____

When?

_____

_____

_____

Things emphasized?

_____

_____

_____

Things repeated?

_____

_____

_____

Cause and effect (if, then, but)?

_____

_____

_____

Things that are alike or contrasted?

_____

_____

_____

_____

TAKING IT ALL IN

Jesus' last words of instruction to His disciples were to prepare them for when He was no longer physically with them. He knew His disciples would need encouragement when He was gone. So He assured them by saying, "The Advocate, the Holy Spirit, whom the Father will send in my name, will teach you all things and will remind you of everything I have said to you" (John 14:26). Then He added that "when he, the Spirit of truth, comes, he will guide you into all the truth" (John 16:13).

If you are a Christian, the Holy Spirit resides in you. With the Spirit as your guide and teacher, are you ready and eager to use what you are learning and dig into your Bible? Hopefully your desire for God's Word matches Job's! He declared, "I have treasured the word of His mouth more than my necessary food" (Job 23:12 NASB).

What Others Have Said About the Bible

*I have for many years made it a practice
to read through the Bible once every year.*

JOHN QUINCY ADAMS
6th President of the United States

7

Are You Seeing It All?

Elisha prayed, "Open his eyes, LORD, so that he may see."
Then the LORD opened the servant's eyes,
and he looked and saw the hills full of horses
and chariots of fire all around Elisha.

2 KINGS 6:17

Recalling their success in the church parking lot the previous week, Justin began this week's meeting by asking Zack, "Do you remember what we talked about in the parking lot last week?"

"Oh, yeah. It was a real eye-opener for me," Zack said with a huge grin on his face. "What you taught me about observation has been very helpful during my quiet times this week. I've been noticing a lot more things now when I read my Bible."

Zack then shared some of the observations he had made. When he finished, Justin complimented him on his newfound skills in Bible study.

"You know, Zack," Justin said, "observation is like playing the role of a detective, like one of those crime scene investigators you see on TV. They go over everything again and again in their search for clues. That's exactly what you are doing as you observe what you are reading. Now that you've gotten a good start, let's move on to the finer points of observation. We're going to go beyond the WH questions and learn how to dig deeper in our quest to get as much as we can out of the Bible."

Observation Requires the Right Attitude

Read 2 Kings 6:14-16. The prophet Elisha is being hunted by the king of Syria, who sends his army to surround the town where Elisha and his servant are staying. The servant panics when he realizes they are surrounded by an enemy force. He asks Elisha, "What shall we do?" How does Elisha respond, and what does he ask God to do for his servant in verse 17?

_____

_____

_____

Observation is most effective when you come to God and ask for spiritual eyes to see. If your attitude is right, God will show you wonderful things from His Word. These steps will help you develop the kind of attitude that will enable you to be more observant as you study your Bible.

1. *Develop a dependence upon the Holy Spirit.* A prayerful dependence on the Holy Spirit is key to all aspects of Bible study, and especially to observation. After each scripture below, write how the Spirit helps you as you read your Bible.

When the Advocate comes, whom I will send to you from the Father—the Spirit of truth who goes out from the Father—he will testify about me (John 15:26).

_____

_____

When He [the Spirit] comes, [He] will convict the world [and you] concerning sin and righteousness and judgment (John 16:8 NASB).

We do, however, speak a message of wisdom among the mature, but not the wisdom of this age or of the rulers of this age, who are coming to nothing. No, we declare God's wisdom, a mystery.... These are the things God has revealed to us by his Spirit (1 Corinthians 2:6-7,10).

Walk by the Spirit, and you will not gratify the desires of the flesh (Galatians 5:16).

I pray that out of his glorious riches he may strengthen you with power through his Spirit in your inner being (Ephesians 3:16).

_____

_____

When he, the Spirit of truth, comes, he will guide you into all the truth (John 16:13).

_____

_____

_____

Can you see why it's so important to come to God's Word with a pure heart—a right attitude? You need all the help you can get when it comes to understanding the spiritual truths in God's Word. You need the Spirit to do His work in your heart as you read. That happens only when you are fully dependent on the Spirit.

2. *Cultivate a willingness to obey.* During your quiet times in God's Word, come to the text with the desire to submit yourself to the Spirit's leading—whatever the cost. This is important because the minute you resist the Spirit's leading is the minute you stop growing spiritually. You must come to the Bible with a desire to learn—and to obey what you are learning.

3. *Train yourself to be patient.* Today, everyone wants instant results. But true learning takes time. You cannot shortcut the process of observation. In personal Bible study as well as in everything else in the Christian life, the process of diligent study is as important as the end product, your spiritual growth.

4. *Develop a scribe's mentality.* In the Bible we read about people called *scribes.* Their job was to carefully record what people said, or to put on paper what they read or observed. As you read

your Bible, that's what you need to do. If you don't write down your observations, you will quickly forget them. So have a note-book, or a file on your computer, or a list on your cell phone where you can record what you observe and learn while you are reading. Then you will have a record to refer back to in the future, a record of your discoveries of God's truths and a record of your spiritual growth.

While writing this book, I have been looking at notes of observations I recorded more than 20 years ago. If the truths are worth the time you spend observing them, then they are worth the time it takes to record them. Unfortunately, a mental obser-vation that is not recorded will soon be forgotten. Don't waste your efforts by relying on mental notes that can easily be for-gotten. Write down your observations so you'll never lose them.

Observation Looks at Structure

When you observe the contents of a Bible passage, you will want to become aware of the form or structure it takes. The writer of a section of Scripture may communicate in any num-ber of forms. Each form needs to be recognized and observed accordingly. Here are some different ways the authors of Scrip-ture communicated God's truth. You've already seen some of this information before, but this time we will go a little deeper.

1. *Teaching*—Jesus used this style in what is commonly called the Sermon on the Mount, which appears in Matthew 5–7. Read Matthew 5:1-10. What teaching technique did Jesus use in these verses? (Hint: Look for repeated words.)

The apostle Paul also wrote the book of Romans in a
teaching style. Paul often used a question-and-answer
teaching technique. What was Paul's question in
Romans 3:1?

_____

_____

_____

2. *Narratives*—Large portions of the Bible are narrative—
that is, they simply tell the stories of what happened to various
people or nations. Many of the historical sections of the Old and
New Testaments (like Genesis to Psalms and most of the Gospels and Acts in the New Testament) are narratives. One nice
thing about narratives is there is no hidden meaning to search out.
The WH questions (Who, Where, When, and What) are helpful
for understanding the flow of the stories found in God's Word.

Read Acts 1:4-5 and observe the story. Also, take a look at
verses 1-3 and 6-9 to see the context—that is, what went before
and after verses 4-5. This will help you with your answers.

Who?

_____

_____

_____

When?

_____

_____

_____

Where?

_____

_____

_____

What?

_____

_____

_____

3. *Parables*—Parables were frequently used by Jesus as an effective way of driving home important spiritual truths. Jesus would talk about a common activity everyone was familiar with—like sowing grain in a field—and related that activity to a key spiritual truth.

The secret to observing parables is discovering the main point and not allowing the many details of the parable to confuse the meaning. With parables, a common mistake is trying to observe too much. Instead, you want to look for the main point.

Look at Mark 4:30-32 and state the point of this parable. (Hint: It describes something about "the kingdom of God.")

_____

_____

_____

4. *Prophecy*—This type of literature deals with future events. Large portions of the books of Daniel and Revelation contain prophetic material. There are other prophetic sections in other

books of the Bible, especially the minor prophets. In many cases the writer who predicts a future event will also describe how it will be fulfilled.

Sometimes prophecies have two parts—a part that will be fulfilled in the near future, and a part that will be fulfilled in the distant future.

Read Isaiah 61:1-2. Then read Luke 4:16-21. What did Jesus say in Luke 4 about Isaiah's prophecy? Also, what did Jesus leave out of Isaiah's prophecy, which predicts what will happen at some time in the future?

_____

_____

_____

_____

5. *Wisdom literature*—Practical advice for living and making decisions is found in Proverbs and some parts of Psalms. Proverbs are short bits of wisdom that deal with daily life issues. If they were written today, they would be called "tweets." A good question to ask of a proverb is, "What does this proverb teach about life?"

What does the following proverb say about a person who listens, learns, and discerns?

Let the wise listen and add to their learning, and let the discerning get guidance (Proverbs 1:5).

_____

_____

_____

_____

The psalms deal mostly with our relationship with God. A good question to ask of a psalm is, "What does this psalm teach me about my relationship with God?"

What do the verses from the following psalm say about God and His dealings with mankind?

> For you are not a God who is pleased with wickedness; with you, evil people are not welcome. The arrogant cannot stand in your presence. You hate all who do wrong; you destroy those who tell lies. The bloodthirsty and deceitful you, LORD, detest (Psalm 5:4-6).

Observation Looks at Key Words

1. *Visualize the verbs.* While observing a Bible passage, it is good to try to discern the action or movement of it. In grammar, action is expressed by verbs. A good way to follow the action is to underline all the verbs in the passage you are studying. Then notice what kinds of actions the verbs are describing. For instance, active verbs have the subject doing the action.

In the verse below, circle the actions the apostle Paul takes in order to be more disciplined:

> I run thus: not with uncertainty. Thus I fight: not as one who beats the air. But I discipline my body and bring it into subjection, lest, when I have preached to others, I myself should become disqualified (1 Corinthians 9:26-27 NKJV).

In your own words, what kinds of actions do the verbs indicate? That is, do you see Paul doing the action, or receiving the action?

_____

_____

_____

Passive verbs have the subject receiving the action. Try this next exercise:

His divine power has given us everything we need for a godly life (2 Peter 1:3).

Who is doing the action described in 2 Peter 1:3?

_____

Who is receiving the action?

_____

What is the result?

_____

_____

Some verbs give commands, which are given either by God or by the writer who is speaking for God. What command appears in 2 Peter 3:18?

Grow in the grace and knowledge of our Lord and Savior Jesus Christ. To him be glory both now and forever!

_____

_____

_____

2. *Picture the illustrations.* Think of a book you read recently that was enjoyable. Why did you like it? Was it the descriptions and illustrations the author used? You probably haven't thought about it, but many of the writers God used to record His Word wrote with word pictures.

Jesus often used illustrations as pictures for His listeners. In your Bible, read Matthew 7:24-27. What illustration did Jesus use to describe a "wise" person who follows His teaching?

_____

_____

_____

How does Jesus illustrate the person who doesn't listen (verses 26-27)?

_____

_____

_____

3. *Concentrate on the connectives.* Words are strung together like pearls on a strand with what are called *connectives.* These connect parts of sentences and paragraphs to each other. Because they are so important, here is a list of connectives and a verse that includes each connective. The translation I used (NASB) for this list may not have the exact same words you find used in your Bible, but you should be able to get the idea.

Temporal or chronological connectives denote time:
after (Revelation 11:11)
as (Acts 16:16)
before (John 8:58)
now (Luke 16:25)
then (1 Thessalonians 4:17)
until (Mark 14:25)
when (John 11:31)
while (Mark 14:43)
where (Hebrews 6:20)

Logical connectives—These connectives are normally found in teaching texts like the book of Romans. They add to the progression of the teaching in basically the same way that a lawyer's argument builds point by point before a jury.

Reason
    because (Romans 2:5)
    for (Romans 1:11)
    since (1 Corinthians 3:3)

Result
    so (Romans 9:16)
    then (Galatians 2:21)
    therefore (1 Corinthians 15:58)—This connective is key and is often used to introduce a summary of ideas. It usually looks back to the preceding sentence, or paragraph, or more.

Purpose
    so that (Romans 5:21)

Contrast

> even though (Romans 1:21)
> but (Romans 2:8)
> much more (Romans 5:15)
> nevertheless (1 Corinthians 10:5)
> otherwise (1 Corinthians 14:16)
> yet (Romans 5:8)

Comparison

> also (2 Corinthians 1:11)
> as (Romans 9:25)
> then as, so through (Romans 5:18)
> in the same way (Romans 1:27)
> just as (Romans 4:6)

Series of facts

> and (Romans 2:19)
> first of all (1 Timothy 2:1)
> last of all (1 Corinthians 15:8)

Emphatic connectives—these are added to make a point or show emphasis, like saying, "Wow!" or "Can you believe it!"

> indeed (Romans 10:18)
> only (Romans 9:10)

I hope these handy tools will help you get started in your understanding of the Bible. Whatever you do, don't get discouraged. Just enjoy discovering your Bible and the many messages God has for you as you grow in your knowledge of Him and follow Him with all your heart.

TAKING IT ALL IN

Observation is hard work and, like any skill, it takes time to develop. You didn't learn to play soccer or baseball or skateboard on the first try. It took lots of practice. And it is the same with observation.

The Bible is a priceless gift from God and is "useful" (2 Timothy 3:16). What else can you say about your daily activities that you would consider "useful"? Probably some aren't all that useful. But when you read and study your Bible you can know and mentally stamp that activity and the time it took as "useful," worthwhile, profitable, a success.

Your life is valuable to God. He has created you, and as His child, He has great things and a great purpose in store for you. Your job is to open your Bible and let Him reveal His plan to you.

What Others Have Said About the Bible

Bible reading is an education in itself.

LORD TENNYSON
Poet Laureate of Great Britain

8

What Does It Mean?

Do your best to present yourself to God
as one approved, a worker
who does not need to be ashamed
and who correctly handles the word of truth.

2 Timothy 2:15

After going over the lesson from the previous week, Justin said to Zack, "Do you remember what I said several weeks ago about the different steps you need to take to understand your Bible?"

Zack scratched his head and, in a halting voice, said, "Uh, observation…interpretation…and…no, don't tell me. I've got it…oh yeah, application!"

Zack was proud of himself, as well he should be. "Congratulations," said Justin. "You now know the essence of how to study your Bible. Now it's time to move on to the next step after observation, or answering the question 'What do I see?' Next let's tackle the question 'What does it mean?'"

Justin went on, "You don't know any Spanish, do you?"

Zack shook his head.

Justin said, "If you don't know Spanish, then how would you understand someone who is speaking in Spanish?"

"I would need an interpreter—someone to explain what that person was saying, right?" said Zack.

"That's right," Justin agreed, "and that's what the next step of interpretation is all about. Interpretation is simply coming up with the plain meaning of a Bible text."

The Plain Meaning

Justin thought for a moment about how to describe "plain meaning," and in a burst of inspiration, asked, "Zack, have you ever read some of the classic youth books like *Treasure Island* or *Two Years Before the Mast*? The reason I mention these books is because of the nature of their stories. They are to be read for their plain meaning. The authors didn't embed hidden or mystical meanings in their books. That's the way you are to read and study your Bible—look for the plain meaning."

And it's true. A good interpreter isn't looking for some unique or hidden meaning in a passage of Scripture. In fact, interpretations that are new or clever are usually wrong.

One example of a wrong interpretation is the use of Bible verses to predict the return of Jesus. Over the last 2000 years, many people have claimed to figure out the date of Jesus' return. But so far, no one has been right. And the amazing thing is that Jesus Himself warned, "About that day or hour no one knows, not even the angels in heaven" (Mark 13:32). The message is that you shouldn't look for some cleaver approach or some hidden meaning in a verse or text.

There are also many people who try to make the Bible support their own opinions. For example, there are people who say the 144,000 souls in Revelation 14 are people selected from their own religious group. These people fail to believe the clear and plain meaning of Revelation 7, which says these 144,000 souls are Jewish evangelists who minister during the Great Tribulation.

Your job as a good interpreter is to make sure your interpretation of God's Word makes good sense and does not contradict other verses in the Bible. And you're not alone in doing this task. God has given you the help of the Holy Spirit, who helps to enlighten you as you do the task of interpretation (see John 14:26).

Maybe you're thinking, *If the plain meaning is what interpretation is all about, then why interpret? Why not just read? Doesn't the plain meaning come simply from reading?*

Yes, in a sense. But in a truer sense, you are dealing with a book that was written thousands of years ago in a different culture. There are two factors you must consider as you look for the plain meaning.

Factor #1: Consider the author's original intent or reason for writing. As we read the Bible, most of us assume that our understanding is in line with what the Holy Spirit is saying or the human author's aim. We can't help but bring our experiences and cultural influences to the text as we read. Sometimes what we bring to the text, though unintentionally, leads us astray or causes us to read incorrect ideas into the text.

Consider, for example, the word "cross" as it appears in Matthew 16:24. What do you think Jesus meant by the following statement?

> Jesus said to his disciples, "Whoever wants to be
> my disciple must deny themselves and take up
> their cross and follow me."

When people in our culture read the word *cross*, they usually think of a piece of jewelry in the shape of a cross. But is that what one of Jesus' own listeners would have thought when he heard Jesus speaking 2000 years ago?

In the first century, when Jesus spoke about the cross, He would have evoked a shocking picture of a violent, degrading form of torture and death that the ancient Romans had perfected into a fine art. The cross was an instrument of shame. Only common criminals or runaway slaves were subjected to this form of death.

So let's return to our question: What would Jesus' listeners think of when He said that in order to follow Him, they would have to take up their cross? They would have realized that following Jesus meant being willing to become an outcast and despised and maybe even die a horrible death.

From this interpretation, you could arrive at this application: How far am I willing to go in order to follow Jesus? Am I willing to follow Him even to the point of death?

Write out a brief statement about the level of your commitment to following Jesus:

_____

_____

_____

Factor #2: Consider the nature of Scripture. Because the Bible is God's Word it has eternal relevance—it speaks to all people, for all times, in all cultures, and has the authority of God behind it.

At the same time, God chose to speak His Word through human beings who made a record of what He said. The words God spoke were meant for the people who were alive at the time, which makes them historically relevant. And His words are also meant for us today, which means your task, as you read and study the Bible, involves two levels of thinking:

- First, you must try to understand the Word of God the way the original readers understood it. You must determine what was said to the original listeners back then and there.

- Second, you must try to understand that same Word of God in the here and now.

For example, let's look at the command in Deuteronomy 22:5: "A woman must not wear men's clothing…" How are we to understand those words?

Taken literally today, in the here and now, it would seem the passage is saying a woman should not wear slacks, pants, or jeans—otherwise she would be disobeying the Word of God. However, if you do careful research, you'll discover that Moses gave this command to the people of Israel because God didn't want the Israelites to follow the practices of the evil people who lived in the Promised Land. He didn't want the Israelite women to copy the pagan women.

So what universal principle was God wanting to teach to the ancient Israelites as well as to us today? He was exhorting them to wear *appropriate clothing*.

If we look in the New Testament, we find another command that fits the interpretation of "appropriate clothing":

> I also want the women to dress modestly, with decency and propriety (1 Timothy 2:9).

Again, as in the Old Testament, the principle is appropriate clothing. This principle is true no matter what era or culture you live in. So the idea of dressing according to God's standards has application for you as well. How should you respond when your parents express concern over your appearance and choice of clothing?

Looking at the Five *C*s

Your goal in Bible study is to determine the plain meaning of the words you are reading. The first task you have as an interpreter is called *exegesis*. This word comes from a Greek term that means to "guide out." This is a careful, systematic study of the Bible that guides you to the original meanings of Scripture.

As in observation, good exegesis comes as you read the text carefully and ask the right questions. Once you have your questions answered, you will be closer to knowing what the author is saying. One very helpful tool for doing this is the five *C*s. They will help you ask the questions that will reveal the author's main thought in a Bible passage.

1. C*ontext* will answer a great many of your questions. In my handwritten notes I once noted a statistic that says "75 percent of all your interpretative questions can be answered by looking at the context." This gives you some idea of how important this *C* is to proper Bible interpretation.

There are two main kinds of context. They are:

Near context—This refers to the verses immediately before and after the verse or passage you are studying.

Far context—This refers to the verses that are farther away and lead up to the passage you are studying, or follow the passage.

So that you can understand how context helps you with interpretation, take a moment to read Mark 1:29-31. Then ask these questions:

Who are the "they" of verse 29? (Hint: the near context—the verses immediately before and after verse 29—will not answer this question. You must look earlier in chapter 1 and search for the far context—see verses 16-20.)

Where or in what city was the synagogue located? (See the far context of Mark 1:21.)

_____

_____

In what region was this city located? (See the near context of verse 28.)

_____

_____

There are different forms of context:

A word—the context surrounding a word is the sentence in which the word appears. Answer this: Whose "house"? (verse 29).

_____

_____

A sentence—the context surrounding a sentence is the paragraph in which the sentence appears. Answer this: Who was sick, and what was her sickness? (verses 29-31).

_____

_____

As you do the task of interpretation, try not to assume even the obvious. Look again at Mark 1:29-31 and, using context, note the verse that answers the question, Who is the "he" in verse 31?

_____

_____

Is context always important? Remember, there are five *C*s you can use to help with your interpretation of Scripture. Context is the first and the most important of these *C*s, for it can answer many of your questions for understanding the author's meaning.

You might be asking, "Are there any passages or books of the Bible where context doesn't apply?" In the book of Proverbs you'll find passages where context is not as important as elsewhere in the Bible. That's because many of the individual proverbs within the book are short, pithy statements that can stand alone, complete in themselves. Many of the proverbs are independent statements of truth that can be understood apart from the verses before and after them.

2. *Cross-references* is the next *C* and refers to letting Scripture interpret Scripture. God does not contradict Himself. One portion of Scripture will never contradict another portion. Your goal is to interpret each passage in the light of the Bible's teaching as a whole. The Bible is one revelation, giving one meaning about God and His will.

You now know about near and far context. When it comes to cross-references, the primary principle is that the whole Bible is the ultimate context of every passage. When you know what other passages say about a subject, you will then be able to gain a better understanding of what specific verses mean or imply.

For example, look at Ephesians 3:14:

> For this reason I kneel before the Father…

If you wanted to answer the question, "What is the correct posture for prayer?" and you happened to read only this partial sentence in Ephesians, you might conclude that because Paul knelt when he prayed, the Bible teaches that you should kneel when you pray. But if you check and cross-reference other verses in the Bible that mention various postures for prayer, you would discover that prayer is also offered while standing, while lying prostrate, or with hands lifted up.

Where can you find a list of scriptures that cross-reference a topic you are interested in or are studying? Zack could turn to Pastor Justin as a resource, and you probably have people you can turn to as well. Ask your youth pastor or Bible study teacher to give you a list of cross-reference verses that will help you when you study a specific passage.

Another helpful resource is a study Bible, which has cross-references in the margin on each page. If you have a study Bible, use it. If you don't have one, ask your parents if they can give you a study Bible for your birthday or Christmas.

Just so you know, there are three other kinds of cross-references. Briefly, they are:

—*Verbal cross-references* focus on the same or similar words that are used in other verses but do not have the same meaning. For instance, Jesus "emptied" Himself in Philippians 2:7 (NASB), yet Ephesians 5:6 speaks of "empty" words.

—*Conceptual cross-references* examine the same concept in different verses using different words—such as when the apostle Paul said basically the same thing in two passages, but chose different words to convey his message. For example, in 1 Corinthians 4:16 Paul wrote, "I urge you to imitate me," and in 1 Corinthians 11:1, he wrote, "Follow my example."

—*Parallel cross-references* present the same event or information yet in different places of the Bible. For example, Acts 9:1-9 describes Jesus confronting Paul on the road to Damascus. In Acts 22:3-16, Paul describes this same event on the Damascus Road.

3. *Culture* helps you understand the Bible from the standpoint of history and geography. The Bible is an ancient book

written in the context of Middle Eastern culture. Interpretation takes into consideration the places where the Bible was written as well as the time period in which it was written.

Geography is important in Bible study. In your Bible, read Galatians 2. What direction did Paul travel to get to Jerusalem?

_____

Geographically, Jerusalem is located on a plateau in the Judean Mountains, and is about 2490 feet above sea level. Any traveler going to Jerusalem from any place in Israel would be required to travel *up* to Jerusalem.

Customs also play a big part in understanding Bible passages. What custom is described in John 13:3-5?

_____

_____

_____

Israel was a dry and dusty land. So when visitors came to your house, it was customary to wash their feet. This duty was usually carried out by a servant. But in John 13:3-5, no servant was available, and none of the disciples were willing to perform this service. Who ended up doing the foot washing? The Lord Jesus Christ. What an example of humility!

4. *Conclusion* is your summary of the meaning of a Bible passage. In this step you state the key thought, or "the big idea," or the main theme of a passage.

In your Bible, review the passages listed below. Then write your conclusion, or what you believe is the main thought of each passage.

Mark 1:29-31

_____

_____

_____

Mark 1:32-34

_____

_____

_____

Mark 1:35-39

_____

_____

_____

5. *Consultation* involves using commentaries, study Bibles, and Bible dictionaries. Commentaries are books written by Bible scholars who explain the background and meaning of the Bible passages you are studying. You will also find similar helpful information in many study Bibles. And a Bible dictionary works just like an English dictionary—it will help you better understand the meanings of words, names, and other things you read in your Bible.

Along with the guidance given to you by the Holy Spirit, these resources will enable you to do a better job of properly interpreting God's Word. Just one note of caution: Try to study each passage yourself *before* you use these reference tools. You want to let the Bible speak for itself as much as possible before you look to resources outside the Bible.

TAKING IT ALL IN

Are you feeling a bit overwhelmed by all that you've read in this chapter? Well, please don't. Understanding your Bible is not something that happens automatically or in just a few weeks or even months. As a Christian, you will be studying your Bible for the rest of your life. And the more you study it, the easier it will become with time and repetition. Keep inching along, and over time, you will see how it influences your life for the better. The Bible reveals the mind of God, and by studying it, you get to tap into His mind each day. Isn't that incredible?

God isn't asking you to become a Bible scholar with several college degrees. But He is asking you to do your best to read and handle His Word correctly. You are wise to begin this process now as a young man after God's own heart. Reading and studying regularly and prayerfully will help ensure that your knowledge of God's Word continues to grow. With that knowledge comes understanding, and with that understanding comes godly living for Jesus.

What Others Have Said About the Bible

A thorough knowledge of the Bible is worth more than a college education.

THEODORE ROOSEVELT
26th President of the United States

9

Digging Deeper

*Now the Berean Jews were of more noble character
than those in Thessalonica, for they received
the message with great eagerness and
examined the Scriptures every day
to see if what Paul said was true.*

Acts 17:11

As usual, Zack couldn't wait to meet with Pastor Justin for their weekly session. He was excited about his progress in learning how to understand the Bible. For the past few weeks, Justin had been teaching the youth group about the ministry of the Holy Spirit. The last time the group met, Justin had taught about the gifts of the Spirit from 1 Corinthians 12. Justin had given a great lesson, and later on that same week as Zack studied the passage on his own, some questions arose in his mind.

"You're going to need a cup of coffee, Justin, because I have a lot of questions for you!" Zack blurted out as he entered Justin's office.

"Uh-oh—I think I've created a monster!" Justin said with a

grin. He then invited Zack to sit down and share what was on his mind.

Zack pulled out the notes he had written during Justin's lesson on the Holy Spirit. Then he pulled out a second set of notes—along with some questions—that he had written while studying 1 Corinthians 12 on his own.

"Zack, you've made my day and my week!" said Justin. "This is exactly what should happen when a person begins to dig deeper into God's Word. I'm thrilled that you are checking out the Bible for yourself—that's exactly what the people in Acts 17:10-11 did."

Digging Deeper

Now it's your turn to do what Zack did. Open your Bible to Acts 17:10-11. Read these verses and put into practice the lessons you've been learning in this book. Remember that to answer some of your WH questions, you will have to go back to the beginning of Acts 17 and read the far context.

Who are the participants?

_____

_____

_____

_____

What is happening?

_____

_____

_____

_____

When is it happening?

_____

_____

_____

Where is it happening?

_____

_____

_____

Now take a look at the context of Acts 17:10-11, or the verses that precede and follow verses 10-11. What is the point of this passage, or the big idea? Your answer will be your interpretation of the Bible text.

_____

_____

_____

What should be the attitude of everyone who hears the Word of God taught? (Hint: What is the title of this chapter?)

_____

_____

_____

How would or could you apply this passage to your life?

_____

_____

_____

_____

Hermeneutics

"Hermen who? Where did this come from?"

If you've never seen the word *hermeneutics* before, you are probably saying, "I thought we were talking about how to study the Bible and the steps of interpretation?"

Well, that's exactly what hermeneutics is all about—this word comes from a Greek term that means "to translate" or "to interpret." This word, in its broadest sense, refers to the science (guided by systematic rules) and the art (skillful application of rules) of biblical interpretation. The goal of hermeneutics is the study of the Bible text in such a way that its original message comes home to the reader or hearer in the context of the here and now.

Jesus, the greatest interpreter and master of hermeneutics, applied this process when He was walking on the road to Emmaus with two men in Luke 24:27:

> Beginning with Moses and all the Prophets, he explained to them what was said in all the Scriptures concerning himself.

What verb is used in Luke 24:27 to describe Jesus' process?

_____

How extensive was Jesus' explanation?

_____

_____

Note: The verb "explained" in Luke 24:27 is the English translation of the Greek word for hermeneutics. Be sure and notice that Jesus was interpreting, for His listeners, what the Scriptures said about Him.

Now read Luke 24:32:

> They asked each other, "Were not our hearts burning within us while he talked with us on the road and opened the Scriptures to us?" (Luke 24:32).

What was the effect of hermeneutics on the lives of the two men who were listening to Jesus?

_____

_____

Looking at the Laws of Interpretation

As you ask questions about the Bible text you are reading, you must make sure you conform to certain rules or laws of interpretation. Just as there are laws of physics and chemistry, there are principles of interpretation that are important for you to follow.

General Principles of Interpretation

Here are some general principles you want to keep in mind as you interpret God's Word:

1. Work from the assumption that the Bible is authoritative and the final court of appeal. The Bible declares itself to be God's Word, and therefore must be obeyed.

2. The Bible interprets itself. Scripture best explains Scripture.

3. Saving faith and the Holy Spirit are necessary for us

to understand and interpret Scripture (1 Corinthians 2:13-14).

4. Biblical examples are authoritative only when supported by a command. Just because Jesus rose early to pray doesn't mean you are required to rise early and pray. While the Bible commands us to pray, there's no specific command about rising early to do that. It would have been different if Jesus had said, "I command you to get up early each day and pray, and if you don't, you are in big trouble!"

5. The promises of God, as found in the Bible, fall into two categories.

> *General promises*—These are given by God to everyone. For example, He causes the sun to rise on the evil and the good, and sends rain on the righteous and the unrighteous (Matthew 5:45).

> *Specific promises*—These are given to certain individuals on specific occasions.

> With that in mind, who is God's promise extended to in Genesis 12:1-3?

Grammatical Principles of Interpretation

The Bible is literature, and proper interpretation requires that you pay attention to the grammatical structure of its words and phrases. Here are some key principles for doing that:

1. Scripture has only one meaning that should be taken normally (the plain meaning). Don't read hidden meanings into the text—they aren't there!

2. Interpret words in harmony with the history and culture of their author.

3. When an inanimate object is used to describe a living being, the statement may be considered figurative and not literal. For example, at the Passover supper, "Jesus took bread, and when he had given thanks, he broke it and gave it to his disciples, saying, 'Take and eat; this is my body'" (Matthew 26:26).

Based on the above principle, how should you interpret this passage? Is the bread literally or figuratively Christ's body?

_____

_____

Jesus also said, "I am the bread of life" (John 6:35). Is this literal or figurative?

_____

_____

What does bread do for a person?

_____

_____

Jesus also said, "I am the gate" (John 10:7). Is this literal or figurative?

_____

_____

_____

What does a gate represent?

_____

_____

_____

Also, when life and action are attributed to inanimate objects, the statement may be considered figurative. Who is the author addressing in Micah 6:1-2 as if they were alive?

_____

4. When an expression is out of character or out of place with the thing described, the statement may be considered figurative.

What animal mentioned in Philippians 3:2 seems out of place and should be considered figurative?

_____

_____

What about the description of Herod in Luke 13:31-32?

_____

_____

5. Parables are illustrations used by a teacher to help explain what he is teaching. A parable is a story, so not every word in the parable necessarily has a special meaning.

Rather, focus on the central idea of the story as a whole to determine the meaning of the teacher's message.

Read the parable of the Good Samaritan in Luke 10:29-37. What question did the man ask Jesus in verse 29?

_____

_____

When Jesus answered the man's question, he offered a parable to illustrate the point He was making.

What question did Jesus ask in verse 36?

_____

_____

Application: Who is your neighbor, according to verse 37?

_____

_____

Historical Principles of Interpretation

History is another important element of proper Bible interpretation. Here are some guidelines to keep in mind:

1. Interpret the Bible in its historical context: To whom was it written? What was the background of the writer? What was the occasion of the writing?

2. God's revelation in the Scriptures was gradually unfolded over time to all people. Both the Old and New Testaments are essential parts of a single unit—the Bible.

The truths that, in the Old Testament, were mysteries have been revealed and made known in the New Testament. For example, read Ephesians 3:1-6. What mystery is explained in verse 6?

_____

_____

Historical facts or events can become *types* or *symbols* of spiritual truths. Who was described as a type or "a pattern" of Christ according to Romans 5:14?

_____

_____

Note: In the Bible, there are very few things or events designated as types or symbols. Romans 5:14 is one of the few declarations of typology. Adam was a type of whom?

_____

Theological Principles of Interpretation

Don't let the word *theological* scare you. Very simply, *theology* is the study of God. So, the things you learn from the Bible about God are what's known as theology. Because every Christian knows at least some things about God, it's appropriate to say that every Christian is a theologian—and that includes you!

When it comes to theology or the study of God, here are some principles you'll want to know or follow:

1. Understanding the Bible grammatically helps you understand it theologically.

2. A doctrine (or teaching) cannot be considered biblical unless it sums up and includes all that Scripture says about it.

For example, consider the doctrine of Jesus' deity, or the fact that Jesus is God. If you were to read John 20:17 in isolation, without looking at any other Bible verses, you might get an incorrect understanding of Jesus' deity. Here, Jesus is talking with Mary Magdalene immediately after His resurrection:

> Jesus said, "Do not hold on to me, for I have not yet ascended to the Father. Go instead to my brothers and tell them, 'I am ascending to my Father and your Father, to my God and your God.'"

Some people use John 20:17 to say that Jesus was not God. But when you look at additional Bible verses, you find clear affirmation that Jesus *is* God:

> No one has ever seen God, but the one and only Son, who is himself God and is in closest relationship with the Father, has made him known (John 1:18).

> I and the Father are one (John 10:30).

> Thomas said to Him, "My Lord and my God!" (John 20:28).

That's why it's important to know what the Bible says as a whole, and not read a verse or two in isolation.

3. When two doctrines (or teachings) presented in the Bible appear to be contradictory, accept both as true in the confident belief that in the mind of God, they are not contradictory but both true. Some examples are:

The Trinity—There is only one God, but the Bible reveals God as being represented in three distinct persons all sharing the same essence, as evidenced in Genesis 1:26: "Let us make mankind in our own image." The words "us" and "our" are plural, which confirms the truth of one God in three persons.

The dual nature of Christ—Jesus is both 100 percent God and 100 percent man. This is confirmed in Philippians 2:5-8: "Have the same mindset as Christ Jesus: Who, being in very nature God, did not consider equality with God something to be used to his own advantage; rather, he made himself nothing by taking the very nature of a servant, being made in human likeness. And being found in appearance as a man…"

God's sovereign election of believers and the free will of man— "He chose us in him before the creation of the world…" (Ephesians 1:4). And, "He is patient with you, not wanting anyone to perish, but everyone to come to repentance" (2 Peter 3:9).

A Passage for Practice

On page 132-133 you will find the text for Acts 16:1-10. It's there so you can try out your new skills of Bible observation and interpretation. Before you look at Acts 16:1-10, here are your instructions. Then, as you read Acts 16:1-10, be sure and check off each part of these instructions as you complete them.

Underline all the verbs. _____ Done

Circle connectives and describe them in the blank margin beside the connectives. Are they temporal, local, logical, etc.? _____ Done

List all the WH questions to ask of this passage, either on the lines below or in the spaces beside the verses.

_____

_____

_____

_____

_____

_____

_____ Done

What's happening along the way?

_____

_____

_____ Done

Where is this taking place?

_____

_____

_____ Done

When is it happening?

_____

_____

_____ Done

How is it happening?

_____

_____

_____ Done

What is the context?

_____

_____

_____ Done

What happened in Acts 15?

_____

_____

_____ Done

How are the people on the missionary team being directed?

_____

_____

_____ Done

TEXT FOR ACTS 16:1-10

1 Paul came to Derbe and then to Lystra, where a disciple named Timothy lived, whose mother was Jewish and a believer but whose father was a Greek.

2 The believers at Lystra and Iconium spoke well of him.

3 Paul wanted to take him along on the journey, so he circumcised him because of the Jews who lived in that area, for they all knew that his father was a Greek.

4 As they traveled from town to town, they delivered the decisions reached by the apostles and elders in Jerusalem for the people to obey.

5 So the churches were strengthened in the faith and grew daily in numbers.

6 Paul and his companions traveled throughout the region of Phrygia and Galatia, having been kept by the Holy Spirit from preaching the word in the province of Asia.

7 When they came to the border of Mysia, they tried to enter Bithynia, but the Spirit of Jesus would not allow them to.

8 So they passed by Mysia and went down to Troas.

9 During the night Paul had a vision of a man of Macedonia standing and begging him, "Come over to Macedonia and help us."

10 After Paul had seen the vision, we got ready at once to leave for Macedonia, concluding that God had called us to preach the gospel to them.

What does this passage tell you about the ministry of the Holy Spirit?

_____

_____

Looking at Acts 16:1-10 as a whole and considering your work in observation and the answers you've written to the questions above, what would you say— in one sentence—is the "big idea"?

_____

_____

_____

How could you apply this "big idea" to your life? What difference should it make in your everyday living?

_____

_____

_____

TAKING IT ALL IN

Look one more time at Acts 17:11. Notice what God said about the Bereans: They "were of more noble character." Other Bible translations describe the Bereans as "fair-minded" or "open-minded." Their willingness to seek out the truth only enhanced their character. Their actions affirm Proverbs 9:9 and its admonition: "Instruct the wise and they will be wiser still; teach the righteous and they will add to their learning."

Now for you, my fellow Bible student. You have embarked upon a noble quest—a quest that few others desire to take. Many people are not willing to pay the price that is required along the way. They recognize that the challenges are great and therefore, they opt not to start the journey. Others start and are quickly distracted and veer off the path, never to return. Those who refuse to make the effort, or who end up falling by the wayside, don't realize that continuing the quest to understand the Bible will yield a life of wisdom and success.

I hope you are already seeing spiritual growth resulting from your quest. But this growth is only the tip of the iceberg. Each day, you are gaining the tools you will need for a lifetime of learning and growing from the Bible. Maybe you have heard this saying before: Give a man a fish and you feed him for a day, but teach a man how to fish and you feed him for a lifetime.

This applies to Bible study as well. When you know how to fish for truth on your own, you are set for life. So hang in there as we learn more about how to study God's Word properly. There are many more fish to be caught!

What Others Have Said About the Bible

Put your nose into the Bible every day.
It is your spiritual food. And then share it.
Make a vow not to be a lukewarm Christian.

KIRK CAMERON, Actor

10

So What Does This Have to Do with Me?

My son, do not forget my teaching,
but keep my commands in your heart,
for they will prolong your life many years
and bring you peace and prosperity.

Proverbs 3:1-2

J ustin and Zack had been meeting weekly for several months, and both had benefitted from their time together. Justin was encouraged to see the excitement in Zack as they made their way through the different aspects of understanding the Bible. Yet Justin knew there was a major step yet to come in Zack's understanding of Bible study.

Up until now, the focus had mostly been on gathering facts— not only facts about passages in the Bible, but also about the unique nature of the Bible. Justin, who was a hunter, knew that the first thing you teach a person who wants to learn how to hunt is the importance of a healthy respect for the hunting rifle. Similarly, the person who wants to learn how to benefit from the Bible must have a healthy respect and reverence for the Bible. Why not? After all, it's the Word of God!

So when Zack arrived for the study time together, Justin asked him to open his Bible to Nehemiah chapter 8. While Zack was thumbing the pages of his Bible, Justin placed a worksheet in front of each of them.

"Zack, we are now in the final stages of learning what is involved in studying the Bible," Justin began. "I want us to work through a Scripture passage that communicates how we are to involve ourselves in the study of the Bible and what the result should be." Printed at the top of the worksheet Justin had created was the title "Nehemiah and Renewal."

Reading for Application

Let's read along with Justin and Zack and learn about the key benefit of studying the Bible. The questions you see below are identical to the ones Justin placed on the worksheet he gave to Zack.

In your Bible, read Nehemiah 8:1-2. As you do so, remember that it's important to note the context of a Bible passage. The context for Nehemiah 8 is this: One year had passed since the rebuilding and completion of the wall around Jerusalem. The people had come together to celebrate a special feast that occurred at this time of the year. When the people assembled, they brought forth a request.

1. Read Nehemiah 8:1-2. What did the people ask Ezra, the scribe, to do?

   _____

   _____

   _____

2. According to Nehemiah 8:3, what did Ezra do, and for how long?

   _____

_____

_____

3. Read Nehemiah 8:5-6. How did the people react as
   Ezra read God's Word to them?

   _____

   _____

   _____

4. What was the people's response, according to verse 9?

   _____

   _____

   _____

5. What action did the people take when they learned
   what God required of them (see verses 14-16)?

   _____

   _____

   _____

6. In the people who listened to "the Book of the Law
   of Moses," the spirit of renewal was not just a brief
   emotional response. Rather, it continued on for
   a whole month. Describe the people's continued
   response to God's teachings in Nehemiah 9:1-3.

   _____

   _____

   _____

Application: Based on what you have just read in
Nehemiah chapters 8 and 9, what should be your
response when you hear God's Word read, taught, and
as you study it yourself?

_____

_____

_____

Responding to God's Word

The people of Nehemiah's day read and studied God's Word,
but their involvement didn't stop there. They responded with
action. The Word of God convicted them of things that needed
changing in their lives—and they obeyed.

That's what the final step of Bible study is all about—applying
God's truths to your life. After you have carefully observed the
verses you are studying, and after you have determined the context and consulted other people and study helps, and after you
have come to understand the proper interpretation and meaning of the verses, then you can answer the question, "How am
I to put this into action in my life?" It is at this point that you
apply what you learn.

Application is the final step of Bible study. As you saw in an
earlier chapter, Bible study is not merely about increasing your
knowledge; it's also about changing your life. You see, the ultimate goal of Bible study is not to do something to the Bible,
but to let the Bible do something to you. The focus of the entire
Bible study process is for you to grow more and more like Christ,
and that requires change on your part.

As with the steps of observation and interpretation, there
is a definite process you can follow to ensure that you apply
the Bible properly. This process builds upon observation and
interpretation:

1. *Starting with the principles of observation, ask your WH questions.* Then ask the following questions to stimulate your mind regarding possible applications:

Is there an example for me to follow?

_____

_____

Is there a promise from God?

_____

_____

Is there a warning to heed?

_____

_____

Is there a command to be obeyed?

_____

_____

Is there a sin to be avoided?

_____

_____

Is there a difficulty with which I need further help?

_____

_____

2. *Use the rules of interpretation.* Apply the five *C*s—Context, Cross-reference, Culture, Conclusion, and Consultation. This is vitally important because personal application cannot happen until you have correctly interpreted the passage and have a right understanding of it. What you believe (interpretation) will determine how you behave (application). It is impossible to behave correctly without believing correctly. Also, there is only one interpretation of a passage, but there may be many applications.

3. *Use self-examination.* By this I mean know who you are as a person—both your assets and your limitations. God has made you just the way you are, so take an inventory:

First, know your assets. Assets are what God has given you. These would be things like talents (such as playing a musical instrument), education (such as speaking a second language), life experiences (such as when your parents take you along when they travel), and your spiritual gifts (these are special abilities given to you by God). As you apply God's Word to your life, you will see how these assets can be used by God for His purposes and to further His kingdom.

Key to knowing your assets is taking the time to list them— not so you can boast about them, but so you know the different ways God can work through you. List some of your assets below, then give thanks to God for these gifts and abilities, and dedicate them to Him.

_____

_____

_____

_____

Second, know your limitations. Don't be discouraged by these supposed liabilities, because God is in control of them. Trust Him for your limitations, and allow them to lead you to greater spiritual growth. Also, your limitations can help develop your faith. For example, maybe you don't have many life experiences because you are still young. Or maybe your physical health is a challenge. Or maybe you don't think you have much to offer. Don't despair! God's Word can give you hope and encouragement as you apply His promises to your life and trust Him.

List your limitations, then thank God for them because they force you to draw on His resources to supply what may be missing in your life.

_____

_____

_____

_____

_____

How can you apply the following verse to your lists of assets and liabilities?

I can do all this through him who gives me strength (Philippians 4:13).

_____

_____

_____

_____

_____

4. *Be selective.* You cannot be consciously applying *everything* you learn, but you can be consciously applying *something*. Select the application that you believe God wants you to work on right now, today.

A good way to be selective is to complete this statement: "My number one problem is _____ ." This will help you identify the most urgent need in your life at this moment. If your heart is open and teachable, God will reveal how the Bible passages you are reading and studying can apply right now in your life!

Look again at 1 Peter 2:1. Which one of these areas of sin do you think God wants you to work on right now?

_____

_____

Next, what will you do now to apply the instruction in verse 2?

_____

_____

Let's say that your number one problem is that you are not sure about God's will or desire for your life. Read 1 Thessalonians 4:3-5 below. What does it say God's will is?

It is God's will that you should be sanctified: that you should avoid sexual immorality; that each of you should learn to control your own body in a way that is holy and honorable, not in passionate lust like the pagans, who do not know God...

_____

_____

There will be times when, as you study the Bible, you might not know what your needs are. According to Romans 8:26, how is the Holy Spirit involved with these unknown needs in your life?

_____

_____

_____

5. *Be personal.* God is a personal God. You can talk to God alone in prayer. You alone must answer to God for your sin. He loves you and cares about you as an individual. Christianity is a personal relationship with God, so when you pray and when you apply God's Word to your life, don't think in terms of *we* or *they*. Think in terms of *I*, *me*, and *mine*. Make it personal.

Look again at 1 Thessalonians 4:3-5 and write out an application using the first-person singular pronoun, *I*, in your application.

_____

_____

_____

6. *Be open to change.* Application is simply the process of relating God's truth to every area of your life with the purpose of being changed. As you consider how to apply the Bible, ask yourself: How does each passage I read or study in Scripture relate to…

…my relationship with God?

_____

_____

_____

…my relationship with others?

_____

_____

…my response to the enemy, Satan?

_____

_____

7. *Act on what you read.* Read James 1:22-25.

What is James's challenge in verse 22?

_____

_____

What is the problem with being only a listener of God's Word (verse 22)?

_____

_____

What happens when you look in a mirror and quickly turn away? If you don't look carefully, you will probably forget or miss something about yourself. According to verses 23-24, how does James apply this analogy to a Christian who does not act immediately after he hears the Word of God?

_____

_____

_____

Contrast this result with the person who is "doing" God's Word (see verse 25). What is the outcome for the person who responds to God's Word?

_____

_____

_____

Try It Yourself

Look again at Mark 1:29-31. What is your interpretation of this paragraph? Or, what was the "big idea"?

_____

_____

_____

For example, your interpretation might be, "Jesus saw a person in need and helped her."

And your application might be, "Hey, I should be willing to help people who have needs," or "I need to watch for people who are in need and offer help to them."

Now look at Mark 1:32-34 and write out your interpretation (the big idea). Then write out your personal application.

Interpretation:

_____

_____

_____

Application:

_____

_____

_____

Next, look at Mark 1:35-39 and write out your interpretation (the big idea) as well as your personal application.

Interpretation:

_____

_____

_____

Application:

_____

_____

_____

Wow—can you imagine living as Jesus did—taking the time to care about people and helping them with their needs?

Maybe you have read these verses before, or heard other similar stories about Jesus. But with your new skills for studying the Bible and your new interest in applying what you are learning, you can better "see" and "hear" God's message to you—and you can choose to actually be "doing" that message. Your choice to do the kinds of things Jesus did in Mark 1 will make you more like Jesus. That, my friend, is the ultimate goal of all Bible study—to become more like Christ.

TAKING IT ALL IN

Application comes in all shapes and sizes. Sometimes your application will require you to do one specific thing, like returning a library book that's been overdue for over a month. It could require you to apologize to your sister for being mean, or to Mom for giving her a hard time. At other times your application will require time and effort, like breaking the habit of lying. It may require taking a series of steps like making payments out of your allowance to replace something you broke while goofing off.

Applications that deal with external actions (like lying, stealing, yelling) can be carried out at any time with an act of obedience, an act of your will. But applications that deal with heart attitudes and motives can be harder to carry out because they require internal change—change in your mind and heart. This kind of change goes deeper and call for you to make right choices in obedience to God's instructions.

Whether you are trying to change your actions or attitudes, here are some suggestions for successful application of God's Word to your life:

1. Write out the issue or problem on an index card and carry it with you as a reminder of what you want to change.

2. Ask God for His help as you work on making that change happen.

3. Memorize key Bible verses that deal with your issue, and obey them.

What Others Have Said About the Bible

Be true to yourself.
Make each day a masterpiece.
Help others.
Drink deeply from good books, especially the Bible.
Make friendship a fine art.
Build a shelter against a rainy day.
Pray for guidance, count and give thanks
for your blessings every day.

JOHN WOODEN
Former championship basketball coach, UCLA

11

The Joy of Discovering Your Bible, Part 1

Your words were found and I ate them,
and Your words became for me
a joy and the delight of my heart;
for I have been called by Your name,
O Lord God of hosts.

Jeremiah 15:16 (nasb)

Justin and Zack sat on the beach looking at the ocean as it took on a bluish-pink hue. The sun was barely beginning to rise over the mountains behind them. They were waiting for it to get light enough for them to hit the surf. As they waited with their surfboards at their sides, Zack turned to Justin and said, "Thanks, Justin."

Justin looked at Zack with a knowing glance, but just to confirm his suspicions, asked, "For what?"

"You know for what, Justin—for teaching me how to understand my Bible. It's hard to say what's been more rewarding... learning from you, or spending time in the Bible."

Justin replied, "You're joking, right?"

"Well, reading and studying the Bible together has been awesome. I can't believe what I'm about to say, but I now actually enjoy studying my Bible!" said Zack.

"Great! And that brings up an important point: Making sure this new habit of studying your Bible continues after we stop our weekly meetings. I have a few more things I want to share during the next couple weeks. But before you start thinking about that—surf's up! Let's go for it!" And off they ran, slamming onto their surfboards as they plunged headlong into an oncoming wave.

Later that week, when Zack arrived at the church to meet with Justin, Justin said, "Zack, before we start, I want to explain where I got the title for these last two lessons. Years ago I read a small book titled *The Joy of Discovery*.[1]

"It made a profound impression on me. It was because of this book—and others—that I came to realize what the joy of discovery was all about when it comes to the Bible. I'm glad to see you too are developing that same joy."

Justin then asked Zack to open his Bible to the book of Jeremiah. "Jeremiah was nicknamed 'the weeping prophet,'" said Justin. "He didn't have much joy in his life because the people of Judah refused to listen to God's warnings about future judgment. For a long time, Jeremiah repeatedly warned of coming doom if the people didn't turn away from their disobedience. Sadly, they turned a deaf ear to the prophet. But in the midst of all his misery and suffering, Jeremiah tells us how he was able to keep on keeping on even though people rejected God's message:

> Your words were found and I ate them, and Your words became for me a joy and the delight of my heart; for I have been called by Your name, O LORD God of hosts (Jeremiah 15:16 NASB).

Read Jeremiah 15:16 again. What two things made real joy possible for Jeremiah?

Jeremiah _____ God's Word.

Jeremiah _____ God's Word.

Jeremiah made the effort to discover what God's Word said. Only after he exposed himself to God's Word did he experience joy. True joy comes in knowing God through His Word. Jeremiah had a desire to know God, and that's the attitude you want to have too!

One Attitude That's Essential

There is one attitude that determines whether you continue to faithfully read God's Word. It's an attitude that will affect your actions for the rest of your life. It is the attitude of desire.

That is, a desire to know God. In order to become a good student of the Bible, you need to learn how to observe, interpret, and apply what it says. And that takes work, as we have seen in this book. But it all starts with having a desire—a true hunger for God that comes from the study of His Word. This desire must come from within you. No parent, youth leader, pastor, or friend can give you this longing. If you have an unsatisfied thirst to know God and His truths, you will read and study the Bible over and over for a greater understanding of God and His message to you. And this unquenchable craving will never stop. It will last for the rest of your life.

In Psalm 42:1-2, how does the psalmist describe his feelings about knowing God?

As the deer pants for streams of water, so my soul pants for you, my God. My soul thirsts for God, for the living God.

_____

_____

What words did the apostle Paul use in Philippians 3:10 to communicate his passion for God?

> I want to know Christ—yes, to know the power of his resurrection.

_____

_____

_____

To know God through His Son, Jesus Christ, you need to desire to understand your Bible, for God reveals Himself and His Son through His Word. This desire is a heart attitude—and it's your choice!

> Ignorance of the Bible means ignorance of Christ.
>
> JEROME, EARLY CHURCH FATHER

Eight Steps to Experiencing the Joy of Discovery

What motivates you to get up early on a Saturday morning to join your team in a soccer match—or to beat the rest of the family to the computer? In a word, it's desire. Within you is a yearning to be the best you can be at something. To fulfill that desire, you have to take steps to make it happen, whether it be getting on the school baseball or track team, or becoming an Eagle Scout.

As a Christian, you should have that kind of desire for knowing God. What are the steps to creating and fulfilling that desire? Here are eight time-tested things you can do to grow in your knowledge of God. A few of these steps will contain bits and pieces of what you've already learned in past chapters, but that's okay! Sometimes we forget what we learn. May God impress these steps upon your heart and mind so they become a lifelong habit for you.

Step 1—Hear the Bible taught. This may seem like an obvious and easy step, but some teens find it hard to do. "What's so hard about hearing?" you might be asking. The challenge for all of us when we go to church is listening carefully when the pastor or teacher speaks. It's so easy for us to get distracted by other thoughts. We end up listening halfheartedly, or not really paying attention. For us to hear the message requires focus. And if you want to remember what you hear, learn to take notes. Come to church or youth group with a notebook and pen, and be ready to write down what you hear.

In Luke 8:11-15, Jesus taught a parable about four kinds of soils and compared these soils to four kinds of responses people have to the Word of God:

> 11 This is the meaning of the parable: The seed is the word of God.
>
> 12 Those along the path are the ones who hear, and then the devil comes and takes away the word from their hearts, so that they may not believe and be saved.
>
> 13 Those on the rocky ground are the ones who receive the word with joy when they hear it, but they have no root. They believe for a while, but in the time of testing they fall away.
>
> 14 The seed that fell among thorns stands for those who hear, but as they go on their way they are choked by life's worries, riches and pleasures, and they do not mature.
>
> 15 But the seed on good soil stands for those with a noble and good heart, who hear the word, retain it, and by persevering produce a crop.

What does a good heart do with God's Word, according to verse 15?

_____

_____

_____

What should your prayer be as you come to church or youth group?

_____

_____

_____

Step 2—Find a time and place to study God's Word. The world is a noisy place. I'll bet as you're reading this book, you can hear cars driving by, the TV blaring, a dog barking, and people talking. It's hard to concentrate, isn't it? Solitude is what you need when you spend time with God through prayer and the study of His Word. Read Genesis 19:27, and list when and where Abraham met with God.

Abraham went early in the morning to the place where he had stood before the LORD (NKJV).

When? _____

Where? _____

According to Psalm 63:1, when did David meet with God, and why? And what was his attitude?

O God, You are my God; early will I seek You; my soul thirsts for You; my flesh longs for You in a dry and thirsty land where there is no water (NKJV).

When? _____

_____

Why? _____

_____

His attitude or desire: _____

_____

What do we see Jesus doing in Mark 1:35?

Very early in the morning, while it was still dark, Jesus got up, left the house and went off to a solitary place, where he prayed.

When? _____

_____

Where? _____

_____

Why? _____

_____

I am not saying you must get up early, nor does the Bible specifically command that. However, it appears from these examples—and this is probably true in your own experience—that if you don't get up a little early each day to spend time with God, you will not get around to reading your Bible and praying. Again, your success in meeting with God goes right back to your desire. How much do you really want to get to know God? It's your choice!

Step 3—Take time to pray. All through the Bible, those who love God are shown as people of prayer. And the same is true all through church history—the greatest men and women of the faith have been people who made a habit of prayer.

Maybe you think prayer isn't all that important, or you think it's embarrassing or a sissy thing to do. But strong men of God are men of prayer. Without prayer, you aren't going to grow in your love and knowledge of God.

Like reading your Bible, prayer is a spiritual discipline. And, like all activities, prayer requires effort. Let me give you some more to think about: If you're not praying—or not praying very much—run through this checklist:

Check your desire. Here we go again—we're right back to attitudes. Prayer will never become a wonderful habit or spiritual discipline if the one main ingredient—desire—is missing. You can know what you should do, and know why you should do it, but if you don't desire to do it, it won't become real in your life.

Check your relationship with God. Is there something that's brought a barrier between you and God? If so, bow your heart and admit it to God. Ask Him to help you do whatever it takes to deal with the obstacles that stand between you and a loving, open relationship with Him—the kind of relationship that enables you to talk to Him about anything and everything, including making right choices.

Check your lifestyle. What—or who—is influencing you? Are you around people and things that can help influence you positively for the things of God? If not, you need to spend more time around such people and things. And if you're influenced by people or things that have a negative influence on your desire for God, then stay away from them. Don't let anyone or anything endanger your relationship with God and your desire to talk to Him in prayer.

Check your understanding. Hopefully you understand that prayer and Bible study are spiritual exercises that require you to be a pure vessel in order to function as God intended. In other words, your life needs to be right before God. If you are hiding sin in your heart, it will inhibit the Holy Spirit's ministry in and through you. Are you allowing wrong attitudes and behaviors to go unchecked in your life? The apostle Paul said we are to get rid of wrong habits. For example, what bad habit is mentioned in Ephesians 4:29?

> Do not let any unwholesome talk come out of your mouths, but only what is helpful for building others up according to their needs, that it may benefit those who listen.

According to Ephesians 4:30, what happens if you refuse to change a habit like this?

> Do not grieve the Holy Spirit of God, with whom you were sealed for the day of redemption.

It's impossible to get spiritual insight and direction when you are grieving God's Spirit through your sin and disobedience. That's why it's important to pray not only before you read and study your Bible, but throughout your day—so you can keep a clean slate with God all the time.

When it comes to prayer, a little bit is better than nothing. Start by praying for a few minutes when you get up each morning. Then get into the habit of saying prayers to God throughout your day. Are you facing a test, a meeting, a sporting activity? Are you having trouble with another student at school? Pray for wisdom for the test. Pray for patience at the meeting. Pray for godly conduct at the sporting event, especially if you lose! And of course, pray for wisdom, patience, and godly conduct when it comes to that problem person at school.

TAKING IT ALL IN

Have you ever gotten lost while out hiking, or gotten separated from your parents at the mall? I once had an interesting experience when I got lost while jogging in Paris, France. I didn't know the language and couldn't read the signs. How did I find my way back to where I was staying? I did two things: First, I prayed for guidance. Second, I started looking for familiar surroundings.

I would like to pass on this same advice to you as you make your way through life. First, seek God's help through prayer not only when you face difficult decisions, but also for your everyday decisions. Ask God to be a partner in all that you do.

Second, when you are not sure what direction you should go or decision you should make, look to God's Word for familiar promises and wisdom. If you are faithful to pray and seek God's guidance from His Word, you can be assured that God "will make your paths straight" (Proverbs 3:6). He will guide you. He will keep you from doing something wrong or foolish. He will guide you into accomplishing His purposes, which are far better than your own! You will become more like the Master and be able to say, "Not my will, but yours be done" (Luke 22:42).

My son, do not forget my teaching,
but keep my commands in your heart,
for they will prolong your life many years
and bring you peace and prosperity.

Proverbs 3:1-2

What Others Have Said About the Bible

*The Scriptures were not given to increase our knowledge,
but to change our lives.*

DWIGHT L. MOODY
19th-Century Evangelist

12

The Joy of Discovering
Your Bible, Part 2

Your words were found and I ate them,
and Your words became for me
a joy and the delight of my heart;
for I have been called by Your name,
O LORD God of hosts.

JEREMIAH 15:16 (NASB)

Have you ever had the feeling that your world was coming to an end? That's how Zack felt as he knocked on Pastor Justin's door for their final meeting. Zack couldn't believe how much he had grown spiritually during the weeks he had been meeting with Justin. He was sad their meetings were coming to an end, but glad for their time together. His life had been going nowhere before this time of learning and understanding how to study his Bible. Now, with his new knowledge and skills, he was beginning to find answers for the things he faced in life and even his future.

Justin opened the door and greeted Zack with his usual smile and look of respect and encouragement. As the two sat down,

Justin gave Zack the second half of the lesson they had started the previous week—which Justin had titled "The Joy of Discovering Your Bible."

"Zack, I'm sure you picked up in last week's lesson that you must possess the attitude of desire if you want to keep moving forward in the habit of Bible study. You will get a sense for the level of your desire once we are done with our discipleship sessions. It's easy for you to stay disciplined when you are accountable to me each week. But what's going to happen when it's just you, your Bible, and God?"

Later that night, after Zack returned home, he reflected on Justin's admonition. Until now, Zack hadn't thought about being self-motivated in his commitment to keep on studying his Bible. The realization was just now dawning on him: What would happen now that he was no longer going to meet with Justin? Would he remain faithful in the habits of prayer and Bible study?

It hadn't been easy for Zack to get up a little earlier each day so he could read, study, and pray. No, the habits had been difficult to develop. Yet through all the struggles, Zack wanted to be able to tell Justin he had done his assignments. That helped to keep him accountable. But would Zack still have the same determination even after he no longer met with Justin?

With these thoughts bouncing around in his mind, Zack looked at the paper Justin had given him earlier that evening. The previous week, they had started looking at the eight steps to experiencing the joy of discovering God's Word. The theme verse was Jeremiah 15:16:

> Your words were found and I ate them,
> and Your words became for me
> a joy and the delight of my heart;
> for I have been called by Your name,
> O LORD God of hosts (NASB).

What did Jeremiah do to experience joy and delight? He found God's Word, and he ate it. That is, Jeremiah personally sought out God's Word and took it to heart. What was the result? "Your words became for me a joy and the delight of my heart."

You, like Jeremiah, must do your part if you want to experience the joy of discovering your Bible. As a child of God, you have the Spirit of God dwelling inside you. The Spirit energizes and equips you as you faithfully follow the steps we are studying. So far we have looked at the first three steps:

Step 1—Hear the Bible taught.
Step 2—Find a time and place to study God's Word.
Step 3—Take time to pray.

Now let's look at the remaining five steps.

Step 4—Read the Bible. Reading your Bible is a simple but effective step in your quest for possessing the joy of discovering your Bible. We've already gone through the mechanics of how to read the Bible. The key is to make it an ongoing habit. Start somewhere in God's Word—anywhere! And stick with it. The only wrong way to read the Bible is to not read it.

According to Deuteronomy 17:19-20, what four things would happen to any future king of Israel when he read God's Word? For your answer, circle each "that" and underline what follows:

> It is to be with him, and he [the king] is to read it all the days of his life so that he may learn to revere the LORD his God and follow carefully all the words of this law and these decrees and not consider himself better than his fellow Israelites and turn from the law to the right or to the left. Then he and his descendants will reign a long time over his kingdom in Israel.

What application can you draw for reasons why you too should want to read your Bible?

_____

_____

_____

_____

What about the different translations of the Bible? The Bible was originally written in Hebrew and Greek. So whatever English-language version you have is a translation of these original languages. Therefore, only the original written manuscript (which we no longer have) is to be considered completely free of translation error. But from the time the original pages were written, scribes and copyists have carefully preserved the Bible by handing down faithful copies of the originals all through the ages, and translators have labored hard to ensure the accuracy of their work. In this way, God has made His Word available in many of the languages people speak today, including English. So don't worry that what you are reading from your version of the Bible might somehow be wrong.

Your decision about which version of the Bible you read comes down to what translation and version is easiest for you to understand clearly. What is the reason for the differences that exist between translations? Here's an overview you might find helpful:

Literal translations—These Bible translations were produced by scholars and translators who, in the translation process, tried to stay as close as possible to the exact words and phrases found in the original languages. These translations are careful to keep the historical context intact at all points. Among the literal translations are the King James Version (KJV), New King James Version (NKJV), New American Standard Bible (NASB), and English Standard Version (ESV).

Free translations—These Bibles aren't actually translations, but attempt to communicate the content of the Bible in a different, simpler way with the reader in mind. A free translation is also called a *paraphrase*. The Bibles usually considered to be paraphrases include the J.B. Phillips New Testament (PHILIPS) and The Living Bible (TLB), and the Message (MSG).

Dynamic equivalent—The scholars who produced these translations focused not so much on word-for-word equivalency, but thought-for-thought. They would translate words, expressions, and grammatical constructions of the original language into concepts more readily understood by readers of the target language. These translations would include the New International Version (NIV) and the New Living Translation (NLT).

While both dynamic equivalent translations and literal translations are useful for Bible study, if you want to get as close as possible to the original meanings of the words and phrases in your Bible, you'll want to use a literal translation like the NKJV or the NASB.

But no matter which you use, the important point is that you take the time to read your Bible—and keep reading it! Dr. Harry Ironside, a respected pastor and Bible student, at age 14, was concerned over not having read through the Bible as many times as he was years old. By the time he was 21 he had caught up. Later in life he was far ahead of his actual age.

As you begin the habit of reading your Bible, instead of starting in the Old Testament, you might want to read a chapter a day from the life of Jesus in either Matthew, Mark, Luke, or John. Those are all good places to start.

Step 5—Study it. It's vitally important that you not only read your Bible, but that you understand it. The book of Proverbs speaks often of finding or getting wisdom. Obviously the wisdom of God is found in the Bible. That's why we study it and dig it out. What do these words from Proverbs 2:3-5 indicate you should do to gain wisdom, and what will happen as a result?

> If you call out for insight and cry aloud for understanding, and if you look for it as for silver and search for it as for hidden treasure…(verses 3-4).

_____

_____

_____

> …then you will understand the fear of the LORD and find the knowledge of God (verse 5).

_____

_____

_____

According to 2 Timothy 2:15, what goal should you have when you study the Bible?

> Do your best to present yourself to God as one approved, a worker who does not need to be ashamed and who correctly handles the word of truth.

_____

_____

_____

When it comes to studying your Bible, there are different kinds of Bibles you will find helpful. First, there are reference Bibles. These will have different tools in them that help you to better understand the text. For example, there are cross-references in the margins on each page, which help you to know other passages you can read to help enhance your understanding. As you take time to read the cross-references, you'll get to know more about the truths and topics found in the passages you are reading.

Then there are study Bibles. These will not only include the cross-references in the margins, but they will also include extra notes and commentary at the bottom of each page. These notes help to provide clarity and insights about what you are reading. If you want to go deeper in your Bible study, ask your pastor or youth leader to recommend a good study Bible. Or go online or to your local Christian bookstore and look at the different selections and layouts, and ask the attendant for their opinion.

Step 6—Memorize it. If you're like most teens, you have no problem at all memorizing the lyrics to your favorite songs. I frequently hear young people singing along as they're walking through the mall or down an aisle at the store. The words are stored in their memories and flowing out of their mouths. Well, that's how easy and natural memorizing God's Word can be, if you choose to make it a part of your life.

Look at these key verses that, when memorized, can help you with making right choices. What does Psalm 119:9-11 tell you—a young person—about a sure way to deal with sin?

9 How can a young person stay on the path of purity?
    By living according to your word.
10 I seek you with all my heart;
    do not let me stray from your commands.
11 I have hidden your word in my heart that I might
    not sin against you.

In your own words, state what God wants you to do about the Bible according to these verses:

Fix these words of mine in your hearts and minds... (Deuteronomy 11:18).

_____

_____

_____

...write them on the tablet of your heart (Proverbs 7:3).

_____

_____

_____

Read Matthew 4:4-10 in your Bible. How did Jesus combat Satan's temptations, and what did Jesus say to Satan when he tempted Jesus in...

...verse 4?

_____

_____

_____

...verse 7?

_____

_____

_____

…verse 10?

_____

_____

_____

What one thing do verses 4, 7, and 10 have in common? Or, how did Jesus combat Satan's temptations—that is, what words did He use?

_____

_____

_____

How can you apply Jesus' example to the times when you face temptation?

_____

_____

_____

Read Colossians 3:16. What do you think is meant by the statement, "Let the word of Christ dwell in you richly" (NKJV)?

_____

_____

_____

Read Psalm 40:8 and write out its meaning in your own words:

I desire to do your will, my God; your law is within
my heart (Psalm 40:8).

_____

_____

_____

I know of no form of intake of the Word
which pays greater dividends for the time invested
than Scripture memory.

DAWSON TROTMAN, FOUNDER OF THE NAVIGATORS

Research is said to show that after 24 hours, you may accurately remember:

- 5 percent of what you hear,
- 15 percent of what you read,
- 35 percent of what you study,
- but you can remember 100 percent of what you memorize.

Step 7—Meditate over it. Meditation is a spiritual discipline. To meditate on the Bible simply means to give prayerful thought to God's Word and how it applies to your life.

Read the three verses below in your Bible. What promises are made to the person who continually meditates on the Word of God?

Psalm 1:1-3—According to verse 3, what promise is given to those who meditate on God's Word day and night?

_____

_____

Joshua 1:8—What promise is given to those who meditate on God's Word day and night?

_____

_____

_____

Luke 6:45—How will meditating on God's Word affect your speech and actions?

_____

_____

_____

Step 8—Live it. The Bible isn't a textbook to be read and remembered just long enough to do well on an exam. God did not give you His Word to simply inform you of facts and information, but to transform you. The purpose of this book about understanding your Bible is to give you tools to understand God's message so you can correctly respond to His will for the rest of your life.

What are the two options you face in your life, according to Romans 12:2?

> Do not conform to the pattern of this world, but be transformed by the renewing of your mind. Then you will be able to test and approve what God's will is—his good, pleasing and perfect will.

Option #1 _____

Option #2 _____

What accompanies your choice of Option #2?

_____

_____

_____

Here are a couple of obvious applications:

—Don't choose option #1. It leads to destruction.

—Choose option #2. Transformation comes as the Holy Spirit changes your thinking through consistent study and meditation on Scripture. The result? Holy living, which God approves.

TAKING IT ALL IN

My persevering friend, you are about to do it—you are almost finished with this book! Thank you for hanging in there. But so far, you have taken only the first step in your quest. Remember what Justin said to Zack: "It's easy to be disciplined when you are accountable to me each week, when there's someone else doing the same thing. But what's going to happen when it's just you, your Bible, and God?"

That's my question for you. What's it going to be for you? How motivated will you be next week or next month to read and study your Bible?

Here's something for you to consider: You will do what you want to do, or what's important to you. And you will do it at whatever the cost and whatever effort is required, right? So what does that say about a desire or lack of desire to read your Bible? If something is important to you, like reading your Bible, then you will find the time, make the effort, and develop it into a habit. So, if you wake up next week or next month and aren't reading your Bible, then evidently God and His Word are not important to you.

I'm hoping and praying this won't be the case for you! I'm praying the information in this book has increased your desire to read your Bible and that you will follow through on the eight steps you've learned so that your Bible study time will be productive, rewarding, and life-changing. May the prophet Jeremiah's words be your lifelong desire: "Your words became for me a joy and the delight of my heart" (Jeremiah 15:16 NASB).

What Others Have Said About the Bible

There are more sure marks of authenticity in the Bible than in any profane history .

SIR ISAAC NEWTON
English physicist and mathematician

APPENDIX SECTION

Introduction to the Appendix Section

To help you continue growing in your Bible study skills, I have added this appendix section. You might want to press on and read this section now, or maybe later when you are ready for some additional encouragement and insights. Either way, don't fail to look it over. You will find this material helpful in your goal of understanding your Bible better.

Appendix 1 is called "A Quick Guide to Bible Study." All the steps on how to study your Bible are summarized here, so if there was something in this book that wasn't clear or you want a quick summary of what you've learned, this appendix will help. If you have friends who would like a copy of this summary, have them go to my website, www.jimgeorge.com, and look under resources to download this overview.

Appendix 2 is entitled "Useful Bible Study Tools." You'll find it fun to familiarize yourself with the many different kinds of Bible study tools and reference materials that can aid you in your study. A working knowledge of these Bible tools will help you enjoy a lifetime of rewarding Bible study.

Appendix 3 is titled "A One-Year Daily Bible Reading Plan."
Throughout this book I stressed the importance of reading your
Bible not just in bits and pieces, but the whole Bible. Very few
Christians have ever read through their entire Bible even once.
Be one of a "few good men" and commit to reading your Bible
through at least once! To help you make this happen, I have
included this reading plan (see pages 193-200). After you finish
each day's reading you can check the box for that day. Here are
some amazing statistics for you, as well as a doable goal:

> It takes 70 hours and 40 minutes to read your
>   Bible out loud.
> It takes 52 hours and 20 minutes to read the Old
>   Testament.
> It takes 18 hours and 20 minutes to read the New
>   Testament.
> It takes less than 12 minutes a day to read your
>   Bible in a year.[1]

Quiet Times Calendar. One of the most important steps to
growing as a Christian is to spend time alone with God each day.
This calendar will help you to do this on a consistent basis. As
you fill in the squares in each column on the calendar, your goal
is for the columns to have a "thermometer look" (filled in completely)—not a "measles look" (with a dot here and a dot there)
or a "Morse Code look" (occasional dots and dashes). You want
to see all the columns filled in as completely as possible so they
show you are making consistent progress in meeting with God.

Appendix 1

A Quick Guide to Bible Study

One of the noblest pursuits a child of God can embark upon is to get to know and understand God better. The best way we can accomplish this is to look carefully at the book He has written, the Bible, which communicates who He is and His plan for mankind. There are a number of ways we can study the Bible, but one of the most effective and simple approaches to reading and understanding God's Word involves three simple steps:

Step 1: Observation—*What does the passage say?*

Step 2: Interpretation—*What does the passage mean?*

Step 3: Application—*What am I going to do about what the passage says and means?*

Observation is the first and most important step in the process. As you read the Bible text, you need to look carefully at what is said, and how it is said. Look for:

- *Terms, not words.* Words can have many meanings, but terms are words used in a specific way in a specific context. (For instance, the word *trunk* could apply to a tree, a car, or a storage box. However, when you read, "That tree has a very large trunk," you know exactly what the word means, which makes it a term.)

- *Structure.* If you look at your Bible, you will see that the text has units called *paragraphs* (indented or marked ¶). A paragraph is a complete unit of thought. You can discover the content of the author's message by noting and understanding each paragraph unit.

- *Emphasis.* The amount of space or the number of chapters or verses devoted to a specific topic will reveal the importance of that topic (for example, note the emphasis of Romans 9–11 and Psalm 119).

- *Repetition.* This is another way an author demonstrates that something is important. One reading of 1 Corinthians 13, where the author uses the word "love" nine times in only 13 verses, communicates to us that love is the focal point of these 13 verses.

- *Relationships between ideas.* Pay close attention, for example, to certain relationships that appear in the text:

  —Cause and effect: "Well done, good and faithful servant; you were faithful over a few things, I will make you ruler over many things" (Matthew 25:21 NKJV).

  —Ifs and thens: "If My people who are called by My name will humble themselves, and pray and seek My face, and turn from their wicked ways, then I will hear from heaven and forgive their sin and heal their land" (2 Chronicles 7:14 NKJV).

  —Questions and answers: "Who is this King of glory? The Lord strong and mighty" (Psalm 24:8 NKJV).

- *Comparisons and contrasts.* For example, "You have heard that it was said...But I say to you..." (Matthew 5:21).

- *Literary form.* The Bible is literature, and the three main types of literature in the Bible are discourse (the epistles), prose (Old Testament history), and poetry (the Psalms). Considering the type of literature makes a great deal of difference when you read and interpret the Scriptures.

- *Atmosphere.* The author had a particular reason or burden for writing each passage, chapter, and book. Be sure you notice the mood or tone or urgency of the writing.

After you have considered these things, you then are ready to ask the WH questions:

Who?   Who are the people in this passage?
What?   What is happening in this passage?
Where?   Where is this story taking place?
When?   What time (of day, of the year, in history) is it?

Asking these four WH questions can help you notice terms and identify atmosphere. The answers will also enable you to use your imagination to recreate the scene you're reading about.

As you answer the WH questions and imagine the event, you'll probably come up with some questions of you rown. Asking those additional questions for understanding will help to build a bridge between observation (the first step) and interpretation (the second step) of the Bible study process.

Interpretation is discovering the meaning of a passage, the author's main thought or idea. Answering the questions that arise during observation will help you in the process of interpretation. Five clues (called "the five *C*'s")can help you determine the author's main point(s):

- *Context.* You can answer 75 percent of your questions about a passage when you read the text. Reading the text involves looking at the near context (the verse immediately before and after) as well as the far context (the paragraph or the chapter that precedes and/or follows the passage you're studying).

- *Cross-references*. Let Scripture interpret Scripture. That is, let other passages in the Bible shed light on the passage you are looking at. At the same time, be careful not to assume that the same word or phrase in two different passages means the same thing.

- *Culture*. The Bible was written long ago, so when we interpret it, we need to understand it from the writers' cultural context.

- *Conclusion*. Having answered your questions for understanding by means of context, cross-reference, and culture, you can make a preliminary statement of the passage's meaning. Remember that if your passage consists of more than one paragraph, the author may be presenting more than one thought or idea.

- *Consultation*. Reading books known as commentaries, which are written by Bible scholars, can help you interpret Scripture.

Application is why we study the Bible. We want our lives to change; we want to be obedient to God and to grow more like Jesus Christ. After we have observed a passage and interpreted or understood it to the best of our ability, we must then apply its truth to our own life. You'll want to ask the following questions of every passage of Scripture you study:

- How does the truth revealed here affect my relationship with God?

- How does this truth affect my relationship with others?

- How does this truth affect me?

- How does this truth affect my response to the enemy, Satan?

The application step is not completed by simply answering these questions; the key is putting into practice what God has taught you in your study. Although at any given moment you cannot be consciously applying everything you're learning in Bible study, you can be consciously applying something. And when you work on applying a truth to your life, God will bless your efforts by, as noted earlier, conforming you to the image of Jesus Christ.

Helpful Bible Study Resources:

Concordance—Young's or Strong's
Bible dictionary—Unger's or Holman's
Webster's dictionary
The Zondervan Pictorial Encyclopedia of the Bible
Manners and Customs of the Bible,
     James M. Freeman

Books on Bible Study:

The Joy of Discovery, Oletta Wald
Enjoy Your Bible, Irving L. Jensen
How to Read the Bible for All Its Worth, Gordon
     Fee & Douglas Stuart
A Layman's Guide to Interpreting the Bible,
     W. Henrichsen
Living by the Book, Howard G. Hendricks

Appendix 2

Useful Bible Study Tools

Try this fun exercise! The good news is it requires no expense on your part. Ask your pastor or youth pastor if you can take a look at their library. (Or you can always visit your public library.) See if you can locate these reference tools that are helpful for when you study the Bible.

1. *Look at a concordance.* The word *concordance* comes from the root word *concord*, which means an agreement between people or, in our case, grammatical agreement. A concordance basically lists every word "in agreement" with every same word used in the Bible. These lists appear in alphabetical order. A concordance shows you every place that a specific word appears in the Bible, usually with a brief quotation showing the context. A concordance can help you locate a verse when you remember only some of the words but not the reference location.

Common English concordances are available for the King James Version, the New American Standard Bible, the New International Version, and the English Standard Version. And the more classic concordances include *Cruden's Complete Concordance*, *Strong's Exhaustive Concordance*, and *Young's Analytical Concordance*.

Which concordances did you find in your pastor or youth pastor's library?

_____

_____

_____

Select one concordance from the shelf and open it up. Suppose you want to learn more about the Ark of the Covenant. Look under the topic heading *Ark*, and see the list that follows. What verses include the word *ark*? (Word of caution: You are not looking for Noah's Ark, but the Ark of the Covenant.)

Which book of the Bible contains the first reference to the Ark of the Covenant?

_____

Which book of the Bible contains the last reference?

_____

Most Bibles have a shortened concordance in the back of the volume. If you are looking for a new Bible to use for personal study, look for one that includes a concordance in it.

2. *Look at topical tools.* One of the best-known topical resources is *Nave's Topical Bible.* This work was the result of 14 years of untiring study by its author, Orville James Nave, and his wife. This tool brings together, in topical form, all the major subjects or topics addressed in the Bible.

Another classic topical tool is *The Treasury of Scripture Knowledge.* It has been available for many years.

Which topical tools did you find in your pastor or youth pastor's library?

_____

_____

_____

In the topical handbook, can you find any references to the Ark of the Covenant? Look at the topics *Ark* and *Covenant*. What did you find?

_____

_____

_____

What additional insight did this tool give you about the Ark of the Covenant?

_____

_____

_____

3. *Look at dictionaries.* Dictionaries fall into two basic categories:

Word dictionaries. You are already familiar with the English-language dictionaries like the various editions of *Webster's Dictionary.* Look up the word *ark* and write a few of its definitions below.

_____

_____

Bible background dictionaries. Two of the popular and widely used Bible dictionaries are *Unger's Bible Dictionary* and the *New Bible Dictionary*. Which ones did you find? If your pastor or youth pastor's library has another Bible dictionary, list it here too.

_____

_____

_____

Look up *Ark of the Covenant* in one of the Bible dictionaries and write out a few notes that detail its construction, where it was placed in the Tabernacle, and where it was moved to at different times in its history.

_____

_____

_____

4. *Look at pictorial Bible encyclopedias.* These are very similar to dictionaries, but usually have more extensive entries and will sometimes include illustrations or pictures. One popular Bible encyclopedia is *The Zondervan Pictorial Encyclopedia of the Bible*. If you find a Bible encyclopedia on your pastor's bookshelves, look at the volume that would include the entry *Ark of the Covenant*. What additional information do you find in the encyclopedia that wasn't in the other tools you've used so far?

_____

_____

_____

5. *Look at historical Bible atlases.* Did you find one or more? List them here.

_____

_____

_____

If the atlas includes mention of the movement of the Ark of the Covenant from where it was originally built in the wilderness until its resting place in Solomon's Temple, trace the journey the Ark took. If you find a map of that journey, that's even better. Briefly chart the Ark's movement:

_____

_____

_____

6. *Look at word studies.* Second Timothy 3:16 says, "All Scripture is God-breathed and is useful." If you want to understand the perspective and background of the ancient Jewish and Christian writers of the Bible, it's important to understand the meanings of specific words used in Scripture. You will find it valuable to know what the words meant in their original usage. Many tools are available to help you investigate the meanings of words used in the Bible. Here are a couple that you can skim through when you have an opportunity to do so:

- *Nelson's Expository Dictionary of the Old Testament* by Merrill Unger and William White

- *An Expository Dictionary of New Testament Words* by W.E. Vine, commonly referred to as *Vine's Expository Dictionary*

7. *Look at surveys of the Bible.* These tools give a brief explanation of each book of the Bible, and also contain brief explanations of selected verses or passages. These fall into three types:

- surveys of the whole Bible
- surveys of Old Testament books of the Bible
- surveys of New Testament books of the Bible

8. *Look at Bible commentaries.* Some Bible commentaries are just one volume, some are several volumes. A commentary will take you verse by verse through a book of the Bible, and offer detailed explanations of the text. Commentaries are more detailed than surveys, and they are usually written by Bible scholars who are very knowledgeable. (Note: The author of a commentary will approach his work from his theological perspective. Before you choose a commentary for your own personal study, be sure and ask your pastor or youth leader for their advice on which ones are the best to use.)

You can also find entire sets of commentaries that cover the Old and New Testaments. For example, there is the *Life Application Bible Commentary* set (by many different authors). There is also *The MacArthur New Testament Commentary* set (by John MacArthur). One popular set is *The Expositor's Bible Commentary*, with Frank E. Gaebelein as the general editor.

What's especially exciting is many of these Bible study tools are now available in electronic form, so you can use them on your laptop or tablet.

All the information you've just learned will give you an idea of the many different kinds of tools that are available for you to use as you grow in your understanding of the Bible. These tools can be useful right now, tomorrow, next week, and next year. As you look for help in digging deeper into God's incredible Word, you'll find Bible study tools extremely useful.

Appendix 3

A One-Year Daily Bible Reading Plan

January

Genesis

- ❑ 1   1–3
- ❑ 2   4–7
- ❑ 3   8–11
- ❑ 4   12–15
- ❑ 5   16–18
- ❑ 6   19–22
- ❑ 7   23–27
- ❑ 8   28–30
- ❑ 9   31–34
- ❑ 10   35–38
- ❑ 11   39–41
- ❑ 12   42–44
- ❑ 13   45–47
- ❑ 14   48–50

Exodus

- ❑ 15   1–4
- ❑ 16   5–7
- ❑ 17   8–11
- ❑ 18   12–14
- ❑ 19   15–18
- ❑ 20   19–21
- ❑ 21   22–24
- ❑ 22   25–28
- ❑ 23   29–31
- ❑ 24   32–34
- ❑ 25   35–37
- ❑ 26   38–40

Leviticus

- ❑ 27   1–3
- ❑ 28   4–6
- ❑ 29   7–9
- ❑ 30   10–13
- ❑ 31   14–16

February

- ❑ 1   17–20
- ❑ 2   21–23
- ❑ 3   24–27

Numbers

- ❏ 4   1–2
- ❏ 5   3–4
- ❏ 6   5–6
- ❏ 7   7–8
- ❏ 8   9–10
- ❏ 9   11–13
- ❏ 10   14–15
- ❏ 11   16–17
- ❏ 12   18–19
- ❏ 13   20–21
- ❏ 14   22–23
- ❏ 15   24–26
- ❏ 16   27–29
- ❏ 17   30–32
- ❏ 18   33–36

Deuteronomy

- ❏ 19   1–2
- ❏ 20   3–4
- ❏ 21   5–7
- ❏ 22   8–10
- ❏ 23   11–13
- ❏ 24   14–16
- ❏ 25   17–20
- ❏ 26   21–23
- ❏ 27   24–26
- ❏ 28   27–28

March

- ❏ 1   29–30
- ❏ 2   31–32
- ❏ 3   33–34

Joshua

- ❏ 4   1–4

- ❏ 5   5–7
- ❏ 6   8–10
- ❏ 7   11–14
- ❏ 8   15–17
- ❏ 9   18–21
- ❏ 10   22–24

Judges

- ❏ 11   1–3
- ❏ 12   4–6
- ❏ 13   7–9
- ❏ 14   10–12
- ❏ 15   13–15
- ❏ 16   16–18
- ❏ 17   19–21

Ruth

- ❏ 18   1–4

1 Samuel

- ❏ 19   1–3
- ❏ 20   4–6
- ❏ 21   7–9
- ❏ 22   10–12
- ❏ 23   13–14
- ❏ 24   15–16
- ❏ 25   17–18
- ❏ 26   19–20
- ❏ 27   21–23
- ❏ 28   24–26
- ❏ 29   27–29
- ❏ 30   30–31

2 Samuel

- ❏ 31   1–3

April		May	
❑ 1	4–6	❑ 1	11–13
❑ 2	7–10	❑ 2	14–16
❑ 3	11–13	❑ 3	17–19
❑ 4	14–15	❑ 4	20–22
❑ 5	16–17	❑ 5	23–25
❑ 6	18–20	❑ 6	26–27
❑ 7	21–22	❑ 7	28–29
❑ 8	23–24		

2 Chronicles

	1 Kings	❑ 8	1–4
❑ 9	1–2	❑ 9	5–7
❑ 10	3–5	❑ 10	8–10
❑ 11	6–7	❑ 11	11–14
❑ 12	8–9	❑ 12	15–18
❑ 13	10–12	❑ 13	19–21
❑ 14	13–15	❑ 14	22–25
❑ 15	16–18	❑ 15	26–28
❑ 16	19–20	❑ 16	29–31
❑ 17	21–22	❑ 17	32–33
		❑ 18	34–36

	2 Kings		**Ezra**
❑ 18	1–3		
❑ 19	4–6	❑ 19	1–4
❑ 20	7–8	❑ 20	5–7
❑ 21	9–11	❑ 21	8–10
❑ 22	12–14		
❑ 23	15–17		**Nehemiah**
❑ 24	18–19		
❑ 25	20–22	❑ 22	1–3
❑ 26	23–25	❑ 23	4–7
		❑ 24	8–10
		❑ 25	11–13

	1 Chronicles		**Esther**
❑ 27	1–2		
❑ 28	3–5	❑ 26	1–3
❑ 29	6–7	❑ 27	4–7
❑ 30	8–10	❑ 28	8–10

Job

❏ 29	1–4
❏ 30	5–8
❏ 31	9–12

June

❏ 1	13–16
❏ 2	17–20
❏ 3	21–24
❏ 4	25–30
❏ 5	31–34
❏ 6	35–38
❏ 7	39–42

Psalms

❏ 8	1–8
❏ 9	9–17
❏ 10	18–21
❏ 11	22–28
❏ 12	29–34
❏ 13	35–39
❏ 14	40–44
❏ 15	45–50
❏ 16	51–56
❏ 17	57–63
❏ 18	64–69
❏ 19	70–74
❏ 20	75–78
❏ 21	79–85
❏ 22	86–90
❏ 23	91–98
❏ 24	99–104
❏ 25	105–107
❏ 26	108–113
❏ 27	114–118
❏ 28	119

❏ 29	120–134
❏ 30	135–142

July

❏ 1	143–150

Proverbs

❏ 2	1–3
❏ 3	4–7
❏ 4	8–11
❏ 5	12–15
❏ 6	16–18
❏ 7	19–21
❏ 8	22–24
❏ 9	25–28
❏ 10	29–31

Ecclesiastes

❏ 11	1–4
❏ 12	5–8
❏ 13	9–12

Song of Solomon

❏ 14	1–4
❏ 15	5–8

Isaiah

❏ 16	1–4
❏ 17	5–8
❏ 18	9–12
❏ 19	13–15
❏ 20	16–20
❏ 21	21–24
❏ 22	25–28
❏ 23	29–32
❏ 24	33–36

❏ 25	37–40
❏ 26	41–43
❏ 27	44–46
❏ 28	47–49
❏ 29	50–52
❏ 30	53–56
❏ 31	57–60

August

❏ 1	61–63
❏ 2	64–66

Jeremiah

❏ 3	1–3
❏ 4	4–6
❏ 5	7–9
❏ 6	10–12
❏ 7	13–15
❏ 8	16–19
❏ 9	20–22
❏ 10	23–25
❏ 11	26–29
❏ 12	30–31
❏ 13	32–34
❏ 14	35–37
❏ 15	38–40
❏ 16	41–44
❏ 17	45–48
❏ 18	49–50
❏ 19	51–52

Lamentations

❏ 20	1–2
❏ 21	3–5

Ezekiel

❏ 22	1–4
❏ 23	5–8
❏ 24	9–12
❏ 25	13–15
❏ 26	16–17
❏ 27	18–20
❏ 28	21–23
❏ 29	24–26
❏ 30	27–29
❏ 31	30–31

September

❏ 1	32–33
❏ 2	34–36
❏ 3	37–39
❏ 4	40–42
❏ 5	43–45
❏ 6	46–48

Daniel

❏ 7	1–2
❏ 8	3–4
❏ 9	5–6
❏ 10	7–9
❏ 11	10–12

Hosea

❏ 12	1–4
❏ 13	5–9
❏ 14	10–14

❏ 15	**Joel**

Amos

❏ 16	1–4
❏ 17	5–9

❑ 18	**Obadiah** and **Jonah**		❑ 10	27–28
				Mark
	Micah		❑ 11	1–3
❑ 19	1–4		❑ 12	4–5
❑ 20	5–7		❑ 13	6–7
			❑ 14	8–9
❑ 21	**Nahum**		❑ 15	10–11
			❑ 16	12–13
❑ 22	**Habakkuk**		❑ 17	14
			❑ 18	15–16
❑ 23	**Zephaniah**			
				Luke
❑ 24	**Haggai**		❑ 19	1–2
			❑ 20	3–4
	Zechariah		❑ 21	5–6
❑ 25	1–4		❑ 22	7–8
❑ 26	5–9		❑ 23	9–10
❑ 27	10–14		❑ 24	11–12
			❑ 25	13–14
❑ 28	**Malachi**		❑ 26	15–16
			❑ 27	17–18
	Matthew		❑ 28	19–20
❑ 29	1–4		❑ 29	21–22
❑ 30	5–7		❑ 30	23–24

October	

				John
			❑ 31	1–3
❑ 1	8–9			
❑ 2	10–11			
❑ 3	12–13		**November**	
❑ 4	14–16			
❑ 5	17–18		❑ 1	4–5
❑ 6	19–20		❑ 2	6–7
❑ 7	21–22		❑ 3	8–9
❑ 8	23–24		❑ 4	10–11
❑ 9	25–26		❑ 5	12–13
			❑ 6	14–16

❏ 7	17–19			
❏ 8	20–21		**2 Corinthians**	
		❏ 3	1–4	
		❏ 4	5–9	
	Acts	❏ 5	10–13	
❏ 9	1–3			
❏ 10	4–5		**Galatians**	
❏ 11	6–7	❏ 6	1–3	
❏ 12	8–9	❏ 7	4–6	
❏ 13	10–11			
❏ 14	12–13		**Ephesians**	
❏ 15	14–15	❏ 8	1–3	
❏ 16	16–17	❏ 9	4–6	
❏ 17	18–19			
❏ 18	20–21	❏ 10	**Philippians**	
❏ 19	22–23			
❏ 20	24–26	❏ 11	**Colossians**	
❏ 21	27–28			
		❏ 12	**1 Thessalonians**	
	Romans			
❏ 22	1–3	❏ 13	**2 Thessalonians**	
❏ 23	4–6			
❏ 24	7–9	❏ 14	**1 Timothy**	
❏ 25	10–12			
❏ 26	13–14	❏ 15	**2 Timothy**	
❏ 27	15–16			
		❏ 16	**Titus** and **Philemon**	
	1 Corinthians			
❏ 28	1–4		**Hebrews**	
❏ 29	5–7	❏ 17	1–4	
❏ 30	8–10	❏ 18	5–8	
		❏ 19	9–10	
	December	❏ 20	11–13	
❏ 1	11–13			
❏ 2	14–16	❏ 21	**James**	
		❏ 22	**1 Peter**	

❏ 23   **2 Peter**

❏ 24   **1 John**

❏ 25   **2, 3 John,
           Jude**

           Revelation
❏ 26   1–3
❏ 27   4–8
❏ 28   9–12
❏ 29   13–16
❏ 30   17–19
❏ 31   20–22

Notes

Chapter 1—Unlocking the Secrets of the Universe

1. H.H. Halley, *Halley's Bible Handbook* (Grand Rapids, MI: Zondervan, 1965), p. 18.

Chapter 2—Do You Have the Code?

1. NIV, NKJV.

Chapter 3—Using Your Secret Weapon

1. Jim George, *A Young Man's Guide to Making Right Choices* (Eugene, OR: Harvest House, 2011).

Chapter 11—The Joy of Discovering Your Bible, Part 1

1. Oletta Wald, *The Joy of Discovery* (Minneapolis, MN: Augsburg Fortress, 1975).

Appendix Section

1. Roy B. Zuck, ed., *The Speaker's Quote Book* (Grand Rapids, MI: Kregel, 1997), p. 38.

Quiet Times Calendar

Jan.	Feb.	Mar.	Apr.	May	June
1	1	1	1	1	1
2	2	2	2	2	2
3	3	3	3	3	3
4	4	4	4	4	4
5	5	5	5	5	5
6	6	6	6	6	6
7	7	7	7	7	7
8	8	8	8	8	8
9	9	9	9	9	9
10	10	10	10	10	10
11	11	11	11	11	11
12	12	12	12	12	12
13	13	13	13	13	13
14	14	14	14	14	14
15	15	15	15	15	15
16	16	16	16	16	16
17	17	17	17	17	17
18	18	18	18	18	18
19	19	19	19	19	19
20	20	20	20	20	20
21	21	21	21	21	21
22	22	22	22	22	22
23	23	23	23	23	23
24	24	24	24	24	24
25	25	25	25	25	25
26	26	26	26	26	26
27	27	27	27	27	27
28	28	28	28	28	28
29		29	29	29	29
30		30	30	30	30
31		31		31	

Date Begun _____

July	Aug.	Sept.	Oct.	Nov.	Dec.
1	1	1	1	1	1
2	2	2	2	2	2
3	3	3	3	3	3
4	4	4	4	4	4
5	5	5	5	5	5
6	6	6	6	6	6
7	7	7	7	7	7
8	8	8	8	8	8
9	9	9	9	9	9
10	10	10	10	10	10
11	11	11	11	11	11
12	12	12	12	12	12
13	13	13	13	13	13
14	14	14	14	14	14
15	15	15	15	15	15
16	16	16	16	16	16
17	17	17	17	17	17
18	18	18	18	18	18
19	19	19	19	19	19
20	20	20	20	20	20
21	21	21	21	21	21
22	22	22	22	22	22
23	23	23	23	23	23
24	24	24	24	24	24
25	25	25	25	25	25
26	26	26	26	26	26
27	27	27	27	27	27
28	28	28	28	28	28
29	29	29	29	29	29
30	30	30	30	30	30
31	31		31		31

Other Books for Young Men by Jim George

A Young Man After God's Own Heart

Pursuing God really *is* an adventure—a lot like climbing a mountain. There are many challenges on the way up, but the great view at the top is well worth the trip. This book helps young men to experience the thrill of knowing real success in life—the kind that counts with God.

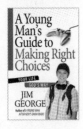

A Young Man's Guide to Making Right Choices

This book will help teen guys to think carefully about their decisions, assuring they gain the skills needed to face life's challenges.

The Bare Bones Bible® Handbook for Teens

Based on the bestselling *Bare Bones Bible® Handbook*, this edition includes content and life applications specially written with teens in mind. They will be amazed at how much the Bible has to say about the things that matter most to them.

About the Author

Jim George is a bestselling author of more than a dozen books and a Bible teacher and Christian speaker. Two of his books were finalists for the Gold Medallion Book Award, *A Husband After God's Own Heart* and *A Young Man After God's Own Heart.* Jim is the author of The Bare Bones Bible® series designed to help readers better understand the Bible. He holds Master of Divinity and Master of Theology degrees from Talbot School of Theology. Jim is married to Elizabeth George, also a bestselling Christian author. For information about Jim's speaking ministry, to sign up for his mailings, or to purchase his books, visit his website at

www.JimGeorge.com

To learn more about Harvest House books and
to read sample chapters, visit our website:

www.harvesthousepublishers.com

HARVEST HOUSE PUBLISHERS
EUGENE, OREGON